IN THE EYE
of the STORM

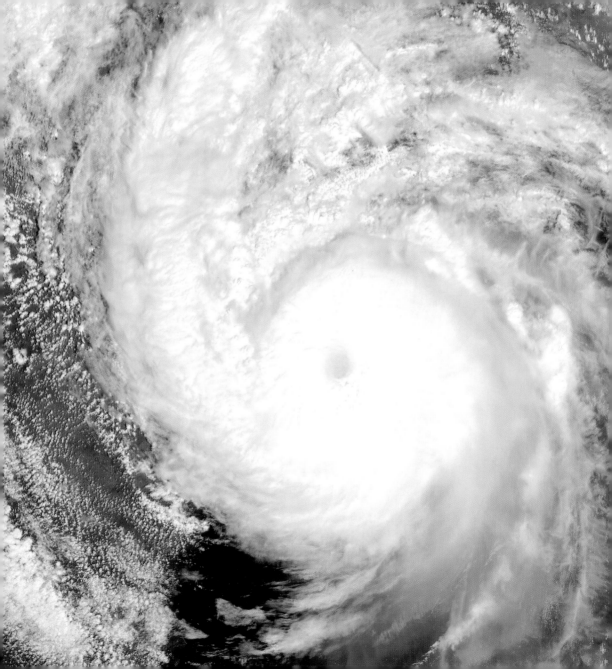

IN THE
EYE *of the*
STORM

WITHSTANDING THE FURY
OF LIFE'S STORMS

ANDY CLAPP

END GAME
Press

In Memory of Ervin Payne—
you always brought calm when storms were raging.

and

To my church family—we have endured so many
storms because the Lord is our foundation.

T A B L E
of C O N T E N T S

INTRODUCTION

a small disturbance develops into a raging storm. Only the Lord knows the extent of the damage that will result.

Just as we experience storms created by changes in the weather, life also produces storms. How prepared are we for the next storm in our life? We feel changes taking place in and around us. Rumbles of thunder reach our ears. The time to prepare is now.

My fascination with hurricanes began in 1989 with Hurricane Hugo. The storm cut a path of destruction from Charleston, South Carolina, through North Carolina and beyond. It affected my hometown. As I attended the University of Mount Olive, we endured numerous tropical storms and hurricanes. Hurricane Fran (1996) and Hurricane Floyd (1999) stand out in my mind over twenty years later. What I noticed was the uniqueness of each storm. Sizes varied. The strength of the storms fluctuated. The duration of each differed based upon the forward speed of the storm.

As I thought about the variances, the uniqueness of each event mirrored the storms of life. Financial, personal, health, career, and mental storms mark our existence. How do we withstand each storm? How can we prepare for a storm with unique features?

Those questions drove me to dig deeper into the Bible. As the year 2020 pounded us with a pandemic, lockdowns, and a flurry of other storms, I wanted to equip people to stand against the onslaught. This devotional emerged from that desire. As Hurricane Laura (2020) approached the coast, I began watching, reading, and writing.

My prayer is that this will give you strength. When life's storms strike, I hope you have a foundation on which to confidently stand. The strength of God's Word provides us the support we need as the storms unleash their fury. The voice of the Lord blankets us with peace even in the chaos of the storm.

A FLOOD
of TROUBLE

"'You speak as a foolish woman speaks,' he told her. 'Should we accept only good from God and not adversity?' Throughout all of this Job did not sin in what he said." *Job 2:10* (CSB)

Will the rain ever stop falling? Each drop adds to the rising waters all around, threatening all we've ever known.

The torrential downpours of Hurricane Harvey (2017) left Houston forever changed. Harvey dropped more than forty inches of rain over a widespread area and caused more than $125 billion in damages. After landfall, Harvey stalled. Storm surge increased the damage. Though the day of the week changed, the storm remained.

The flood waters destroyed lives and property. Entire neighborhoods sustained damage. Harvey's impact continued even after the waters receded. The memories of the storm linger even today.

During the onslaught, the storm pointed to Job's story.

Job endured an extended storm. With each wave, he suffered. The oxen and donkeys were stolen by the Sabeans, who killed all but one servant caring for those animals. Lightning struck all his sheep and all but one of the servants tending the sheep. Chaldeans took the camels and killed his servants there, but one. Then, his children perished when the house collapsed. The thought "At least I have my health" lasted only a moment. Plagued by boils, he scratched himself with shards of pottery to find relief.

The suffering, however, gave way to rejoicing. God blessed Job. Job held tight in the storm and God rebuilt his life afterward.

Job was a righteous man. Had life presented a reason for him to complain? Absolutely. Yet he asserted to his wife that they must accept the good and the bad. He remained steady in the storm. As everything threatened his way of life, he kept his eyes on the Lord.

At the conclusion, God restored everything. Job 42:12 (csb) says, "So the Lord blessed the last part of Job's life more than the first." Job remained with God. God remained faithful to Job.

Some storms hit consecutively. One setback is followed by another suffering. The year 2020 felt like such a storm. Before we caught our breath from one storm, another made landfall. For most, 2020 featured one long cyclone of struggle.

As certain seasons of life prove harder to endure, righteousness beckons us to stand firm. A storm subsides eventually. A season passes at some point. And though today brings overcast skies, a new day awaits.

The sun rises again. The clouds move. Even more important, the Son is risen, so what we face today becomes more manageable in light of the resurrection of Jesus Christ. We can praise God even in the middle of the storm because He is bigger than the storm.

As the storms bear down, press in harder to the Lord. Instead of focusing on the fury, focus on the deliverance. Job's story instills hope in the raging storm. His story implores us to hold to faith and anticipate brighter days.

The presence of the Lord is with us during the storm, and He will be present after the storm.

When all seems to be washing away, praise Him for what remains. See what you have that cannot be lost rather than seeing only what has been lost. Praise Him in the pouring rain. Sing a hallelujah even in the strongest surge of the storm. Raise your hands to heaven when the floodwaters of life rise.

God is still God. You are not alone, nor do you face this storm alone. In the middle of a storm is the perfect time to praise the Lord.

Storm Preparation

- What can you praise Him for today?

- What will you raise your hands to praise the Lord for at this moment?

- How does praising God help us when we are facing the storms of life?

- How does Job's story help you?

2

A STORM
of DOUBT

"Immediately Jesus reached out His hand, caught hold of him, and said
to him, 'You of little faith, why did you doubt?'"
Matthew 14:31 (CSB)

*W*hat if I don't make it through? What if I lose everything?
A moody storm pressed northwest towards the North Carolina
coast in 1996. Hurricane Fran experienced changes in the open waters, yet it
intensified before striking North Carolina. Fran struck as a major hurricane,
making landfall near Cape Fear, North Carolina.

As a sophomore at Mount Olive College, I chose to stay, to ride out the storm.
Other friends made the same choice, but they lived near the coast from child-
hood, so they knew what to expect. Curiosity directed my decision-making. The
initial thrill of a storm approaching, however, deteriorated as quickly as the conditions outside. By 1 a.m. I silently doubted we would survive the night. The
intense pressure of the storm caused the apartment building to creak. The wind

tore the siding away, each piece clanging as it flew through the breezeway and off into the night.

Doubts arise in life. The wondering about our survival howls in our minds like gale-force winds.

The initial fear of Christ's appearance amidst a howling storm gave way to boldness for one of the twelve disciples. "Call me out there, Jesus," Peter shouted. Jesus called back. Courage filled Peter, and a timid first step became a journey to Jesus on the open water. All the others stayed in the boat. Peter stepped out.

Trouble arose once the emboldened follower shifted his focus. Peter took his eyes off Jesus. His courage crumbled when he looked at his own ability and the circumstances swirling around him. Doubts led to fear. And fear nearly led to a drowning.

On his own power, Peter's first step would have resulted in his sinking. The fact he reached as far as he did on the open waters revealed the power of Christ. A normal man stepped out into the unknown as if it were natural. Yet, he took his eyes off how far he came in Christ and doubted what he could do on his own.

Just the slightest shift sank the disciple. He no longer heard the voice of Jesus, He listened to the voices inside that said, "You'll never get there. You will perish. Man wasn't made to walk on water." The wrong voices pulled him down and, in a moment, Peter went from standing tall to slipping beneath the waves.

Panicked, he flailed his arms wildly. Crying out, he admitted his need for a Savior. Thankfully, the Savior stood on the waters nearby. Jesus reached out and took hold of the one who took his eyes off Jesus seconds earlier. When we read Peter's story, we see how doubts affect every life, including ours.

Uncertainties storm into our lives. What begins with one doubt intensifies into a hurricane of questions and reservations that leaves us sinking when we once stood on a solid foundation. One hesitation pondered too long sets us up for failure.

Voices proclaim we cannot do what we are doing, or we are under-equipped to accomplish what we need to do. Failure seems probable rather than merely possible. We are reminded of past failures. Others might ridicule us, especially if we fall. These doubts begin the downward spiral of a life called to walk on the water.

Storms arise when we focus only on what we can do, neglecting to believe what the Lord can do. If we assess only what we think we have, we face endless limitations. His power stands unrivaled and limitless. As the Lord has proven over time, He can do what man believes to be impossible.

The world tells us the first step to success is to believe in ourselves. Those words seem encouraging, but truthfully, we need to believe in more than ourselves. Our faith in God, and in His ability, silences the storm of doubt. Faith reminds us that God can do what we cannot. He holds the power to change lives, open doors, and overcome the very obstacles we face.

Replace the phrase "I can't" with "God can." When the impossibilities of life arise, turn to the confidence we have in the Lord. When storms of doubt threaten you, remember what the angel spoke to a young girl given life-altering news. As Mary wondered how, Gabriel promised, "For nothing will be impossible with God." (Luke 1:37 csb)

On your own, doubt says the storm is impossible to survive. With God, we know the impossible becomes possible.

Storm Preparation

- How did Peter's doubts disrupt his journey on the water?

- What are some of your doubts in life right now?

- How do you combat doubt and ride out the storm of doubt in life?

- Gabriel's words to Mary gave inspiration. Why do those words matter to us when we face death in life?

3

A STORM
of FEAR

"Then they all deserted Him and ran away." Mark 14:50 (CSB)

h urricane Hugo (1989) approached the United States with a fury few had witnessed. It arrived as a Category 4 storm at landfall. The eerie hours leading up to its direct hit injected fear into the lives of the residents of North and South Carolina. The size of the storm engulfed two states. The strength promised catastrophic damage. No one knew what might remain after the storm passed. The unknown gripped the hearts of those in the path.

To see the radar images today, over thirty years after the storm, we recall the fear of those days. As a pre-teen, I faced such a storm for the first time.

Fear arises when the unknown confronts us.

What will the result be?

What will happen to me in this storm?

One time we see such a fear in the Bible is in the response of the disciples to Jesus' arrest in the garden. He warned them the day would come. More than once He said these events loomed on the horizon.

But fear overtook faith when the moment came. A mob approached. Their courage fell. They followed Him for three years, but where He was going that night they were not prepared to go. So, fear kicked in and they abandoned the One who never abandoned them. An angry mob drove the disciples to run away. Mark pointed out how they deserted Jesus in the moment He needed them most. So scared was one person that his garment came off and he kept going, never pausing to retrieve his clothes. A storm brewed that night in the garden and those with Jesus ran away for self-preservation.

Fear led Peter to deny Him repeatedly later. Unease locked the disciples in a room after the death of Jesus. It was anxiety that led the women to carry spices to the tomb because they expected Him to be dead. They assumed He was wrong about a resurrection.

Life features storms of fear from the time we are born until the day we draw our final breath. Children cry out in the night, unsure of what might lurk in the darkness. Adolescent life breeds fear of ridicule and anxiety about what path to choose after graduation. Later, fears of finances, health, family, and broken friendships mark the landscapes of life.

The world presents plenty to be suspicious of every day. We long to know what will come, so the idea of the unknown threatens our inner core.

Scripture calms our fears if we immerse ourselves in the Word. Isaiah captured these words from the Lord. "Do not fear, for I am with you; do not be afraid, for I am your God. I will strengthen you; I will help you; I will hold on to you with My righteous right hand." (Isaiah 41:10 CSB) Fear appears in the face of the unknown. Faith triumphs when we know God, to Whom there is no unknown.

The Lord told Joshua not to fear as he assumed the role of leadership. The Lord said, "Haven't I commanded you: be strong and courageous? Do not be afraid or discouraged, for the Lord your God is with you wherever you go." (Joshua 1:9 CSB) The time and situation offered reasons for Joshua to worry, but the Lord gave him a bigger reason to have faith. The Lord promised to be with him.

A storm of fear begins with a single event. A doctor reveals a bad test result. A company warns of layoffs. A threat is made. The market collapses. A single event triggers a swirling storm of fear.

But here's how we endure the storm. Remember, the Lord holds you. Fears diminish in the face of the protection of the Maker of heaven and earth. Rather than holding on to the unnerving, take hold of the hand that holds on to you. Fear not! The Lord is with you. Let God take care of it. He promises help, strength, and His presence.

As the storm of fear rages, we go back to the words of Psalm 56. It says, "When I am afraid, I will trust in You." (Psalm 56:3 CSB) Putting trust in the Lord comes from a heart of faith.

These are the storms that drive much of the direction of a life. We avoid what frightens us. We yearn for safety. You are safe in the arms of the Lord. The disciples learned that lesson after the Resurrection. The ones who fled later faced persecution and death with an unshakable faith.

Storm Preparation

- Where is fear driving your life right now?

- How can growing in your faith help you to overcome your fears?

- What do we learn from the change in the disciples' lives?

- Why should you trust God when facing the unknown?

ALERT:
A STORM
is COMING

"Make yourself an ark of gopher wood. Make rooms in the ark and cover it with pitch inside and outside." Genesis 6:14 (CSB)

*t*he warning reached the ears of more than three million people. Enormous Hurricane Floyd approached the southeastern shores of the United States. A warning pressed the masses to flee, which many did as they made their way inland. Local news outlets, the Weather Channel, and national news reports painted a dire picture. The alerts pushed residents and vacationers to take action. Though some refused to budge, the largest evacuation in United States history (at that point in 1999) took place. Cars lined the highway. Busy beach communities became ghost towns.

This storm was unlike other storms, and those who heeded the warnings signed in relief that they listened. Power outages left many areas in the dark. In some, a foot of rain fell, flooding roads and isolating those who chose to ignore the advance warnings. Those who fled found the safety they needed.

In life, there are warning signs. Whether we pay attention and heed the warnings is ultimately our choice. Those who dismiss the warnings often find themselves in a state of regret, while those who listen find themselves filled with thankfulness.

Just as those who heard the alert and took action, Noah received a warning and undertook preparations. God told him to build an ark. The Designer of life provided specifications on the design of the vessel. God explained that a flood loomed on the horizon.

Noah trusted God though he held no knowledge of what the flood might present.

God warned that the heavens would open up like never before. Noah faced the choice—listen to God and live or doubt God and take his chances. He listened. He embraced the warning, and his decision impacted his family. The design of the ark ensured that Noah and his family safely lived through the storm. And amazingly, if you read the story of Noah, it was God who sealed the ark, ensuring it was closed up in such a way that Noah and his family would survive the coming flood.

Others saw the ark yet remained unmoved. How can anyone see such a massive vessel and fail to question if they, too, should make preparations? Inevitably, some commented that Noah had lost his mind. The world scoffed but ultimately perished. Creation failed to see what the Creator could do.

Do we hear the Lord as He warns a storm is heading in our direction? Do we see God as an advance warning system?

Think back through Scripture for a moment. God warned Noah. Through the interpretation of Pharaoh's dream, Joseph passed on God's revelation that a famine loomed. Jesus told of an impending storm. He told of His crucifixion before His hour came. His instructions in the Garden of Gethsemane pointed to a storm brewing. He told the disciples, "Stay awake and pray so that you won't enter into temptation. The spirit is willing, but the flesh is weak." (Mark 14:38 CSB) The Lord has always tried to stir creation to pay attention, but few heed the warnings.

Be alert. Storms threaten throughout life. Calm waters become raging seas in a matter of minutes. Some storms have warning signs while others develop out of nowhere. Those who stay alert find a greater preparation when the storms strike. And know this—no storm catches God off-guard.

Though we are caught off-guard by the events of life, God is never shaken. He knows what's coming. Often He speaks beforehand to prepare us, just as He did with Noah. Being in tune with God—having our ears open to hear the warning—helps us to be ready for what we never saw coming.

Storm Preparation

- Where is God showing you that a storm could arise in your life?

- What actions are you taking to be ready if the storm takes aim at you today?

- How can you better listen to God to receive His alerts today?

A STORM
of OPPOSITION

"Then Jesus said to the chief priests, temple police, and the elders who had come for Him, 'Have you come out with swords and clubs as if I were a criminal?'" Luke 22:52 (CSB)

*W*hat do you do when you feel like life is collapsing on every side?

In September 2004, Hurricane Frances made landfall in Florida. Hutchinson Island became the point of landfall but with the size of the storm, residents hundreds of miles away endured Frances' wrath. A Category 2 storm, the story of the hurricane extended well beyond its wind speeds and storm surge. Frances spawned over one hundred tornadoes that tore through the Southeast. The fury of the storm made an impact deep into the Mid-Atlantic states. The Eastern Seaboard took a hit from every angle.

The twisters forced people from Florida to Virginia to keep an eye out as one could touch down at any time. The unpredictability of a hurricane grew even more unpredictable with the flurry of tornadoes dropping randomly from the sky.

We have seasons where it feels like the world stands against us. Times of uncertainty rattle the depths of our souls as we wonder what may come next. Conditions deteriorate, clouds form, and trouble brews. We feel the fury in full force.

But we are not the only one who face such a day. Jesus knows what it's like to endure a storm of opposition.

The cross loomed. After the Upper Room, Jesus and the disciples walked to the Garden, Jesus aware of what approached. When the opposition arrived to arrest Jesus, they came as a mob, wielding swords, torches, and clubs. As the crowd drew near, even Jesus noted the force with which they showed up. The mob sent terror into the lives of the disciples and, as Mark noted, they fled. The numbers, the fury, and the realization that He was one step closer to the cross made for a lonely moment for the Lord.

Righteousness matters. Righteousness on display faced a mob in the Garden of Gethsemane in the person of Jesus. With a word, the mob could be struck down. With the swipe of His hand, the threat of the mob could be handled forever. But the will of the Father held Jesus' obedience. Rather than give in to the flesh, He chose to remain in righteousness by going where the Father called Him to go. Righteousness is doing what is right, even if it is painful or inconvenient. A storm unleashed its rage, but Jesus had what it took to stand.

So much can be learned from Jesus. His resolve in the face of opposition teaches us how to stand when the world is crashing down around us.

Storms of opposition come in life. As they arrive, we face a choice—run with the masses or do what's right. Do we live cautiously to lessen any opposition even if means we fail to do what is right? The answer to what we should do in a storm of opposition comes from Jesus' example and from Paul's letter to the Galatians.

Paul knew the gospel faced opposition. He lived that reality. For the Galatians to stand, they needed wisdom to stand on. He wrote, "For am I now trying to win the favor of people, or God? Or am I striving to please people? If I were still trying to please people, I would not be a slave of Christ." (Galatians 1:10 HCSB)

Tornadoes may spin all around you. The howling voices shout out against you. The rain and floods of life threaten your very existence. Keep standing. Let Paul's words to the Galatians keep you focused and allow Jesus' example to give you the strength you need to withstand the storms of opposition. Standing for truth and standing for the Lord will put a bulls-eye on you, but Jesus shows us the storm can be withstood.

The storm will pass. In the meantime, make sure your witness stays intact as the storm of opposition rages.

Storm Preparation

- How does Jesus' response to opposition give you strength?
- Where are you battling opposition in your life right now?
- How can you better handle opposition in a godly way?

A STORM
of TEMPTATION

"After the Devil had finished every temptation, he departed from Him for a time." *Luke 4:13 (CSB)*

*i*f we ponder it long enough, we convince ourselves it won't be that bad.

A hurricane drew closer to the coast of North Carolina in 2020. More powerful storms hit the state in the past, so the initial fear was minimal. Many assumed the storm would be a simple nuisance, so they chose to ride it out on the coast. Just prior to landfall, the temptation to stay turned into a regrettable decision as Isaias intensified as the pressure dropped and the winds increased. The lure that it was "not that bad" became "worse than we thought."

The images shocked those who thought the system was to be a minor issue for a night. Images of the surge and the winds filled many live feeds on social media. Isaias proved that storms, especially hurricanes, should always be taken seriously. That hurricane, which many thought would be forgotten soon after it dissipated, is now a storm referenced when discussions start about the 2020 hurricane season.

Temptation came like a storm to Jesus. The Bible tells us He fasted forty days prior to the strike of Satan and when the Devil came, he attacked the weakest area. The deceiver tried to manipulate Jesus to turn stones into bread. Weak from hunger, easily He could have given in. Instead, Jesus revealed what fed Him—the Word of God.

Satan attacks us in the same manner that he initiated the temptation of Jesus. The weakest parts of our lives bear targets for which he aims. Do you struggle with lust? Images immediately appear on your computer or television. Do you struggle with regret? He'll remind you of every time you made a mistake. What you may have forgotten, he will dig up and remind you of at every turn. He knows our weaknesses and strikes that spot first.

Temptation intensifies just like the hurricane off the Carolina coast. "Not so big" morphs into a bigger danger than we once thought it to be. One temptation whirls into a barrage of enticements, all with an expressed desire to make us fall. Satan whispers, "It's not that bad" only for us to see later that the cost of the sin was "worse than we thought." He thrives on lies but even in the storm of temptation, we have somewhere to turn. There is a calm in the eye of this onslaught.

Finding peace in these particular struggles begins with a turn to the Lord. Retreat to prayer when the storm rages. Dive into the Word of God when a flood of temptation rises. Trade the howling winds of temptation for the sound of praise in Christian music. Rather than fixating on the temptation, set your eyes and your mind on the things of God.

Paul reassured the Corinthian people that they were not doomed to be overtaken by temptation. The city of Corinth's reputation told that temptation abounded. Yet Paul encouraged them. He wrote, "God is faithful, and He will not allow you to be tempted beyond what you are able, but with the temptation, He will also provide a way of escape so that you are able to bear it." (1 Corinthians 10:13 HCSB)

There is a way of escape available to us every day. Jesus used scripture to overcome the temptation of Satan. Instead of staring at temptation, perhaps we should look around to find an escape route that God has provided. Temptation marks every stage of life, but the power to stand against the storm of temptation changes the way we look back and view the stages of our lives. To withstand and remain steadfast in our conviction means less regret later down the road as we avoided the pitfalls of thinking something wouldn't be "that bad."

Storm Preparation

- What are the weak areas in your life right now? How can Satan attack you in those areas?

- What are you doing today to prepare for the storms that could arise tomorrow?

- How do you react when temptation arises? What changes can you make to help you withstand the storm of temptation more successfully?

A STORM *in* RELATIONSHIPS

"When the ten disciples heard this, they became indignant with the two brothers." *Matthew 20:24 (CSB)*

*i*s there trouble brewing? Are there signs that the storm is growing as a threat?

A multitude of elements come into play in a hurricane. A tropical wave serves as the starting point, what forecasters note as they determine which waves have the potential to further form. Water temperatures dictate the ability of a storm to grow. The position and strength of other pressure systems and storms determine the direction. If everything lines up right, a storm can be sent out to sea without a landfall. But any opening, even the smallest shifts, opens the door for a storm to strengthen and strike, leaving devastation behind.

2020 now stands as the most active season on record. Twenty-nine named storms threatened coastal residents. The year featured one storm after another, an unrelenting barrage of watches and warnings. At one point, so many systems spun in the Atlantic that memes were created about a "Hurricane Train." Few took their eyes off the tropics, not wanting to be caught off-guard.

There are certain seasons where all the elements are in place for trouble. In those seasons, our eyes are alert to take note of any potential issue.

Storms in relationships originate in much the same way. Something happens. A minor disagreement or a breakdown in communication churns up the once peaceful waters in the relationship. A small storm intensifies. If left unaddressed, that storm makes landfall in our lives and unleashes havoc. Before we know it, if not handled, one storm follows another, each one weakening the foundation of a relationship.

The disciples spent so much time together. Just as any group that spends excessive time together, a small disagreement can become an overwhelming annoyance. The mother of the sons of Zebedee asked Jesus for esteemed positions for her sons in eternity. The request led to bickering and grumbling among the disciples.

As the disciples bickered, the heart of the argument was *their* place. Their frustration rose from a place of pride and self-interest. Each thought they deserved a prime spot next to the Lord. Yet, Jesus fixed the issue. By revealing the false mindset of the world, Jesus opened the eyes of His followers to His way of thinking.

Jesus explained the greatest position a person should strive to fill. Of all the places, where Jesus pointed was least desirable. He took the argument then transitioned it from one between the disciples to the power structure of the Gentile world. He explained how the Gentile world used power to lord over people. Then, Jesus talked about how His followers were to be different, just as He was different from every other king in the world. He explained that the greatest were the ones who took the place of a servant. He spoke of the very role He would assume when He went to the cross.

Wants caused frustration, bickering, and threatened the relationships, even of the disciples. Just as it did the day the mother of the sons of Zebedee made the request, many storms in relationships develop when we forget to set aside our wants. Jesus repositioned the eyes of the disciples off of what they could get and on to what they could give. His guidance laid the groundwork to stronger relationships.

Relationships are stronger when the approach is "what can I give" rather than "what can I get" or "what I deserve." The elements arise for a storm of destruction when we only think of ourselves. Selfishness stirs up storms in relationships as one person tires of the expectation to constantly fulfill the other's wishes. When we refocus, when we set aside our wants and will, the storm can dissipate. It begins by listening to the words of Jesus and setting aside ourselves for the sake of another. Such a move forces the storm to move out to sea, no longer a threat to the stability of the relationship we hold dear.

Storm Preparation

- How can you become a better servant in your life?

- Why does an attitude of servanthood strengthen a relationship?

- How does the sacrifice of the cross challenge you to be more servant-minded?

A STORM
of GUILT

"He asked him the third time, 'Simon, son of John, do you love Me?'
Peter was grieved that He asked him the third time, 'Do you love Me?'
He said, 'Lord, You know everything! You know that I love You.' 'Feed
My sheep,' Jesus said." *John 21:17* (HCSB)

*g*uilt comes in the recognition that more could have been done.
    Hurricane Katrina devastated New Orleans at landfall. A Category 5
storm, Katrina hit with a vengeance. Reportedly, fifty-three levee breaches
occurred, allowing the water to spill into the city. The rushing waters claimed
the lives of many residents, the winds tore apart structures (including the roof of
the Superdome), and the horrors of the moments replay in the minds of many
with the mere mention of the storm's name.

    In the aftermath of Katrina, many felt the pains of guilt due to the cata-
strophic loss of life and property. What could have been done to evacuate
people beforehand? How could the levees have been updated in anticipation

of a storm of this magnitude? Why hadn't preparations happened in advance?

Unfortunately, nothing erased the reality of what unfolded. All that could be done was pick up the pieces, repair what was broken, and prepare for what could be in the future. Despair in the aftermath led to a storm of guilt and second-guessing

Peter felt unrelenting guilt as he stood before the Lord after the Resurrection. Before the cross, while in the Upper Room, the outspoken disciple swore he would never deny Jesus. He could not imagine any scenario that would cause him to turn his back on Jesus. Not only did he swear he would stand firm, but he even took it a step further. Peter assured that he would die for Jesus before He would deny.

In the safety of the Upper Room, his words came easy as his confidence ran high. Yet, when he witnessed Jesus' arrest, fear set in, and his actions failed to follow his earlier proclamation. He fell not just once, but three different times.

As Jesus stood before Peter after His victory over the grave, He asked if Peter loved Him. Not just one time did Jesus ask the question of the future leader of the church. Jesus asked three times. For each previous denial, Jesus gave Peter a chance to change his earlier decision. Jesus knew the magnitude of Peter's calling and knew that guilt promised to impede Peter's progress in the kingdom work.

Peter's future wasn't erased by his past. As he confessed his love for Jesus, Jesus turned Peter's guilt into a new life. From that point forward, Peter's life made waves for the gospel.

Satan reminds us of all we did wrong. He hopes we'll focus on what cannot change so we abandon the work of changing the world. Guilt floods our lives too often. We have our defenses built up, but with one little reminder of a mistake of the past, all the guilt floods in again and wrecks us. But God's forgiveness turns our cry of guilt into shouts of praise. You are forgiven. You have new life! Rather than live in regret, we turn to the Lord for restoration!

Storm Preparation

- Where are you struggling with guilt today?

- What do you need to lay down from the past so you can move forward in the present?

- How does Jesus' response to Peter help you embrace His forgiveness?

A STORM *of* DISAPPOINTMENT

"Then Martha said to Jesus, 'Lord, if You had been here, my brother wouldn't have died.'" *John 11:21* (CSB)

*h*ere we go again.

The city of Lake Charles, Louisiana, found itself in the news more than it wished to be in 2020. Lake Charles garnered the attention of the nation. Weather Channel reporters set the scene as Category 4 Hurricane Laura approached. Though thirty miles inland, the city suffered a massive strike as winds up to 128 mph shredded roofs and toppled buildings. The late August storm left its mark on Lake Charles.

Afterwards, rebuilding began. Each step brought a glimmer of hope, but six weeks later, trouble brewed in the Gulf of Mexico. Hurricane Delta struck, making landfall only twenty miles from Laura's strike, and again, Lake Charles took a direct hit. Though this storm wasn't as strong, Laura's impact weakened structures and trees, making them vulnerable to more damage even in a weaker storm.

Disappointment marked the lives of many.

One storm was bad enough.

A second strike overwhelmed.

If only the storm trekked fifty miles east, the damage would have been lessened. If only the storm had dissipated, less would have been completely destroyed.

Disappointments are a part of life. They come and they leave marks. "If only" becomes the song of those singing the woeful tune of disappointment.

Martha and Mary felt the storm of disappointment. Their storm began with despair as their brother, Lazarus, struggled to hold on to life. His condition worsened, and a few days later, he passed. Despair gave way to disappointment, however, when Jesus arrived.

"If only You were here," a broken soul said as He approached. The sisters sent word to Him earlier, when Lazarus fell ill, when, in their minds, something could still be done. If anyone could do anything, He could. But His coming was delayed and, when Jesus finally arrived, her disappointment could not be contained. Martha's emotions revealed how the events rocked her.

A few moments later, her sister approached. "If You had been here," she said, her words an echo of her sister's remarks to Jesus. Mary uttered the words through her tears, her pain pouring forth from every pore of her body. Both struggled with the fact that a different outcome could have transpired if only Jesus arrived sooner.

Their brother's death opened the door for a miracle to unfold. A storm of disappointment gave way to a new day with three words of Jesus: "Lazarus, come out!"

Setbacks descend on a daily basis. People let us down. Life fails to bring about what we long to experience. A shattered dream lies in ruins. We fail, which leaves us disappointed in ourselves, and what we hope for falls short of our expectations.

Though we know that the letdowns are part of life, what do we do when they come?

Proverbs 24:16 tells us to get up when we get knocked down. The despair of disappointment gives way to hope when a resilient spirit exists within us. Repeatedly, the Bible implores us to persevere. Today is a new day and, though yesterday brought its share of disappointments, there is hope in just a few words of Jesus.

Storm Preparation

- What effect does disappointment have on you?

- How can you better overcome disappointments?

- How does the story of Lazarus, and the feelings of Mary and Martha, give us hope in the face of disappointments in life?

A STORM *of*
DISRUPTION

"Then the angel told her, 'Do not be afraid, Mary, for you have found favor with God. Now listen: You will conceive and give birth to a son, and you will call His name Jesus.'" *Luke 1:30–31 (HCSB)*

*a*t moments, in some entire seasons, life fails to go as planned. Even the most detailed plans need room for disruption.

Jurassic Park stands as one of the most iconic movies of all-time. The dinosaurs and the storyline captivated audiences throughout the world as the realistic-looking beasts came to life on the big screen. Though nearly everyone knows of the movie, few know of the storm that interrupted filming. As the film reached the last days of production, a storm unleashed its fury. Hurricane Iniki (1992) struck as one of the strongest hurricanes to hit the Hawaiian Islands where filming took place.

The storm-packed winds of over 140 mph, destroying the island of Kauai (plus major damage to nearby Oahu) and ripping apart many of the sets for the movie. Iniki interrupted life and altered the landscape. Residents faced rebuilding their homes and their lives. Plans for the future gave way to massive disruption, an altering of dreams, a devastation unplanned. Residents rebuilt. The people persevered. The film crew pitched in and cleared roadways. A devastating storm struck but, much like a movie, life had to go on.

We plan much of life. But there are times when life alters those plans. Storms arise and throw the order of life into chaos. What do we do when disruptions occur? Our answer dictates our direction in life.

Mary had her life planned. A wedding celebration awaited. She and Joseph mapped out their future, but with Gabriel's visit, that life was put on pause. A heavenly interruption forced Mary to face an unknown when she received her calling in life.

Questions swarmed moments later. Though she knew the truth, relaying that truth promised difficulties. Would Joseph believe her? Would she even live to see her Son be born? All the plans she had before evaporated. What she expected faced disruption.

She humbled herself and accepted a new plan. She focused on what God called her to do instead of dwelling on the disruption of the day. God revealed a massive variant in her path and that change unlocked an even greater existence.

God altered her plans. His reasoning stands as a gift to Mary, to Joseph, and to the entire world. She thought she knew what the future held, but God knew her future before she drew her first breath. The diversion from her script made all the difference.

Disruptions are sure to happen. They come in different sizes, some a mere blip while others are a complete overhaul. Do you give up when life doesn't go as planned? Do you sulk when dreams lie in the ashes of a disruption?

The show must go on. Faith tells us God has a reason and, even in the interruptions, we can grow and tell a bigger story as a result. Mary continued down the road God called her to walk. It wasn't the same as her original plan. When an unplanned change comes in life, pause to see what God is doing. Take a moment to investigate if it's a temporary pause or a complete redirection. Remember what He told the children of Israel in Jeremiah 29:11. The Lord said, "For I know the plans I have for you." Sometimes, He has to disrupt our plan, so we begin to follow His.

Storm Preparation

- How does Mary's response to disrupted plans encourage you today?

- What can disruptions provide to you that is a positive?

- Why is it important to keep going forward in the wake of a storm of disruptions?

A FINANCIAL STORM

"One of the wives of the sons of prophets cried out to Elisha, 'Your servant, my husband, has died. You know that your servant feared the Lord. Now the creditor is coming to take my two children as his slaves.'" *2 Kings 4:1 (CSB)*

One of the costliest storms in American history affected millions up and down the Eastern Seaboard in 2012. Superstorm Sandy disrupted life and dealt a major blow to New Jersey. Images of flooded areas of the Garden State pointed to catastrophic damage and financial ruin. The diameter of hurricane-force winds extended 1,150 miles, and costs exceeded 65 billion dollars in the United States alone.

The storm struck people from all walks of life. Republicans and Democrats assessed the damage which affected the rich and the poor, business owners and employees, and the young and the old. Thriving areas sat underwater, and emerging from the troubles took years.

One storm. Areas less prone to substantial hurricane damage found no safe harbor as the superstorm lashed out. No one imagined the financial turmoil at the beginning of October, but November revealed financial struggles on a massive scale.

Most of us live paycheck to paycheck. We tuck away a little here and there but truthfully, one major hit and a financial flood threatens to wipe us out. A sickness drains away every penny and leaves us overwhelmed by debt. An injury robs us of our ability to do the job that we've been doing for years. The loss of a job creates a void as missing or reduced income fails to meet what the bills demand.

A woman in the Old Testament experienced this truth. Her husband died in debt, leaving her a widow and broke. Creditors indicated they would take her children to reclaim the debt, so she cried out to Elisha. She had nowhere else to turn.

Her husband hadn't planned for a day when he wouldn't be around. Now, she faced even more loss…for a wife and mother, it would be a total loss. She turned to Elisha and God provided. Elisha told her to borrow containers and to fill them with the jar of oil she had.

She did what he told her to do. The oil flowed until the last container was full. With the abundance provided by the Lord, she had enough to pay the creditors and keep her sons. As the Lord blessed in excess, she had enough to live off of after that day.

Two lessons come from her hurricane. The first truth comes from her husband and his lack of forward-thinking. He left behind a financial mess as he failed to manage life properly on earth. His short-sighted decisions endangered his wife and sons. The false belief that there would always be more time or opportunities to get caught up was a grave miscalculation.

Our second truth comes from the wife. As financial storms strike, trust in the Lord and do it God's way. He's able. He can provide and, sometimes, we have to put our trust that He will provide, even if His way doesn't quite make sense to us in the moment. The widow in the temple highlights this truth. She placed in the offering plate two mites. It was all she had but she trusted that the Lord was able to take care of her needs.

Financial storms strike. Prepare today and handle it God's way.

Storm Preparation

- What can we learn from the husband's decisions?

- How does the faith of the widow inspire you today?

- Why is it important to think long-range about finances for your family?

A HEALTH STORM

"A woman suffering from bleeding for 12 years, who had spent all she had on doctors yet could not be healed by any, approached from behind and touched the tassels of His robe. Instantly, her bleeding stopped." *Luke 8:43–44 (csb)*

*W*hat can this lead to?

What is lurking underneath?

Flood waters present more dangers than most think about. Floods wash away cars, pose dangers from downed power lines, sweep people away to drown, and inundate properties. Hurricane Matthew in 2016 brought enormous rainfall amounts. A steady flow from the heavens washed out roads in Haiti and in the United States, but another danger lurked in the aftermath—illness.

Flood waters sweep across saturated lands. The waters carry with them various germs that contaminate water supplies in areas devastated by flooding. Drinking water serves up glasses of sickness. Puddles offer a breeding ground for mosquitos to multiply and spread sickness. Matthew's flooding posed threats to public health in ways most never thought about.

The danger of some storms is that they start within. Their origins are not immediately recognizable.

A storm's impact can be more than a situation. It can affect your condition, your overall health. So many of us have battled illness and sickness. Sometimes, those storms feel overwhelming.

A lady's story appears in Luke. Though we know her condition, he never mentions her name. Her storm, however, was one of her health, and she pressed in to get within reach of the Source of help.

For twelve years she suffered before that day. Her desire to overcome, to find relief, left her drained financially and still battling sickness. Only One solution remained. She needed Jesus. The Great Physician stood in a massive crowd, but the obstacle before her didn't deter her. She pushed further. She reached out harder. The hand of the hurting reached for the robe of the Healer. Nothing stopped her from touching His robe because He was the only hope she had.

Storms on our health strike. They come in spurts, and they can define entire seasons of our lives. A season of contending with ill health disrupts all of life. We struggle to do what once we accomplished effortlessly. But God is there to help you.

Sickness and health issues will come. Whether it be a passing illness, or something deemed terminal, illness will confront each of us. Because of the fallen nature of man, we endure storms which assail our health.

But the illness, even if terminal, is not the end of the story. There is more. Though sickness unleashes ruin on our health, Jesus promises eternal healing in Him. Though we may not be healed on earth, eternal healing comes from Christ.

Revelation 21:4 declares that, in heaven, the tears are wiped away from our eyes. The pains of this life are forever erased, and sickness no longer has a grip on us. John wrote it this way: "He will wipe away every tear from their eyes. Death will no longer exist; grief, crying and pain will exist no longer, because the previous things have passed away." (Revelation 21:4 HCSB) We inherit a new body that never wears out; joints that never break down.

A place of healing awaits in eternity. Even in the throes of sickness, we can endure knowing the storm will pass one day, and eternity promises perfect health when we truly arrive at home. No more pain. No more grief. What a day it will be when we get to heaven!

Storm Preparation

- Why should we praise the Lord even in sickness?

- How does the thought of heaven help us along the way?

- How does the woman with the hemorrhage teach you to press into Jesus?

A LINGERING STORM

"The flood continued for 40 days on the earth, and the waters increased and lifted up the ark so that it rose above the earth." Genesis 7:17 (CSB)

Some parts of life seem to creep along. Though we wish it would hit and move on, these trials linger around far longer than we desire.

Though it wasn't quite a storm of biblical proportions, to many, it felt the same. Hurricane Florence (2018) crept towards the North Carolina coast, dousing the area with rain and eroding the coast with winds and storm surge. The storm struck just south of Wrightsville Beach.

The system slowed to speeds of five miles per hour in its approach, allowing the outer bands to continuously churn out water. As it made landfall, the system slowed even more. Spinning over the Old North State before dipping into South Carolina, Florence barely moved. Rainfall amounts climbed into the double digits in inches and hour after hour, the forecast remained the same—rain and wind. Elizabethtown, North Carolina, recorded nearly three feet of rain in the storm.

ABC 11 in Raleigh reported on the event, keeping the public aware of all developments. The decision was made to cover the storm without interruption. Due to the speed of the hurricane, this "story" extended longer than anyone initially imagined. Seventy-five hours of continuous news spoke to the lingering nature of Florence over the Carolinas. There were points when everyone wondered if and when it would ever end.

Some storms move so slowly. Hour after hour becomes day after day and the consistent condition is rain pouring down. Those inside such storms wonder if it will ever pass. They question if they should adapt to the struggle as that appears to be their new reality.

Can you imagine how Noah and his family felt? Talk about lingering storms! For nearly six weeks, the rain fell. As each day passed, the waters rose. An ark full of animals stunk and, through it all, there was only more water.

Hope remained in the drabness of forty days of rain. Though they struggled to see light at the end of the path, Noah's family knew the very boat they boarded was a bright spot. The rains came, just as God revealed beforehand. The flood waters rose, and with so much precipitation, the inevitable happened. Destruction unfolded as humanity perished. But for Noah and his family, the Lord had made a way.

The forewarning of God told what to expect. The guidance of God showed Noah that God had made a way. As God foretold of a storm of forty days, He assured Noah that it would one day subside.

Are you in a season of perpetual rain right now? Does every day look overcast as you struggle to get through another week? The storm will pass. God knows when it will subside, and He hasn't left you alone in the storm. What He has done for you is what He did for Noah and Noah's family. He made a way for them, and He's made a way for you!

It reminds us of what Jesus said to the disciples just before the cross. He promised that the coming storm would pass. He said to them, "So you also have sorrow now. But I will see you again. Your hearts will rejoice, and no one will rob you of your joy." (John 16:22 HCSB)

Look up today and, even if it remains overcast, praise Him that this storm will pass. He made a way for you through Jesus, and, in Christ, the clouds begin to break because we know the Son has risen.

Storm Preparation

- How important were God's instructions to Noah prior to the flood?

- Why is it hard to praise in a lingering storm?

- What impact does it have on you to know that God has made a way for you?

THE
AFTERMATH

"Though a righteous man falls seven times, he will get up, but the
wicked will stumble into ruin." *Proverbs 24:16 (HCSB)*

*a*monster storm promised carnage as it drew near Homestead, Florida,
in 1992. Hurricane Andrew uncorked a fury Florida had never seen
before. The Category 5 hurricane tore through the Sunshine State, leveling
entire communities as it featured sustained winds of greater than 150 miles
per hour and gusts of over 170.

Pandemonium ensued in a hurricane of such force. So many images remain
fresh in the minds of those who lived through it and those who watched
in horror from afar. The aerial views showed neighborhoods flattened.
Homestead Air Force Base resembled a place that fell victim to a bombing.
The signs warning looters to stay away made the news. Yet, other signs issued
a call to persevere. Throughout the area, signs promised, "We will rebuild."
The storm hit with all it had. The people refused to stay down, rising back up

to put their lives back together. Such a spirit inspires us even today, as we look back thirty years after the storm.

Life will present storms. What we do after tells the story about what exists deep within us.

Paul faced a storm nearly non-stop after he encountered the Lord on the road to Damascus. Yet he refused to give up. In writing to the believers in Corinth, Paul inspired those who endured storms in life and in faith.

Paul wrote, "We are pressured in every way but not crushed; we are perplexed but not in despair; we are persecuted but not abandoned; we are struck down but not destroyed." (2 Corinthians 4:8–9 HCSB) Paul points to the storms but gives hope. He had been beaten down but, through the power of Christ, he stood back up. Then, he inspired with these words, "Therefore, we do not give up. Even though our outer person is being destroyed, our inner person is being renewed day by day." (2 Corinthians 4:16 CSB) Storms threw all they had at the apostle but, in the aftermath, he only grew stronger.

His example gives others hope that they can endure what life brings. The power of God superseded all that Satan attempted, and Paul pushed others to weather their storms by relying on the Lord in the process.

In the aftermath of the storms of this life, we have two options—get up or give up! We can bemoan what happened, living in the destruction, or we can celebrate its passing and rebuild with great determination. We rejoice in the faithfulness of God, and we reflect on how He moved. We emerge with an attitude of gratitude and a greater appreciation for the Lord…and we get back to work. There is more to be done.

Storms strike your life. The pain of the storm continues to sting. Life shook in the storm, and there may even be parts of life that collapsed. But you have today. As Psalm 118 says, "This is the day the Lord has made; let us rejoice and be glad in it." (Psalm 118:24 HCSB) The Lord gave you today, this very breath, and an opportunity to get up, dust yourself off, and move forward. There is more to your story yet to be told. The Lord has more to do with your life!

Paul said, "Don't give up." Proverbs said, "Get back up." The Lord assures us that there is more to be done even in the aftermath of a storm, and, through His power, there will be a story of His faithfulness to come.

Storm Preparation

- What is your normal reaction in the aftermath of life's storms?

- How does Paul's writing to the Corinthians inspire you today?

- Why is it important for Christians to get up after a storm strikes in life?

15

A RESTLESS STORM

"In the evening of that first day of the week, the disciples were gathered together with the doors locked because of their fear of the Jews. Then Jesus came, stood among them, and said to them, 'Peace to you!'" John 20:19 (HCSB)

*t*he time crawls as we await the impact.

Sometimes, no one knows what to expect. Even with all of our forecast tools available today, a storm in the ocean remains temperamental and goes in whatever direction it chooses.

A system approached the Eastern Seaboard in 1999, barely missing the Outer Banks of North Carolina. Rather than continuing on, the atmosphere shifted, leaving the storm adrift in the Atlantic. Before long, the near miss became a direct hit as Hurricane Dennis turned and headed back toward North Carolina. The path of the storm shows a loop and an initial near miss that only gave a short relief.

The storm remained restless as it moved inland. As the storm jumped around, the nerves of those possibly in its path remained on edge. Would the storm strike their area? How much damage might result?

The trepidation in the face of that hurricane is indicative of large portions of our lives.

Panic and restlessness come in the face of that which is out of our control. Long nights result from our overactive minds. Fear rises from imagined outcomes based on what could be.

The events of Thursday and Friday shook the disciples. After the Lord's Supper, a storm struck, led by one of their own (Judas Iscariot), and swept up their Leader. As the mob arrested Jesus in the Garden of Gethsemane, they ran away, fearing for their own safety. Crucified on a cross, Jesus' fate shook the disciples in such a way that they tried to avoid being seen. Locked away, the nights grew longer as restlessness rose.

Their world spun out of control. None of the disciples held the power to do anything. The body of Jesus lay secured in a tomb. Minds raced as they feared the coming days. Friday night crept by. Saturday seemed endless and as a result, they struggled to rest. What might be gave birth to images of severe persecution and possible death. But the restlessness eventually ended in an extraordinary way.

All the doors were secured out of fear of religious leaders barging in to take them captive. The room was full of anxious followers, some of whom paced. Some stared into the distance. Then, He appeared. Without a knock. Without opening a door. In the center of the room stood the Hope that calmed their souls in a way that only the Lord could.

We, too, struggle with unknowns and situations out of our control.

Restlessness creates long nights as our minds shuffle through images of worst-case scenarios. We think of what we can do. We devise a plan as to what we will do if everything falls apart. We outline every scenario possible to ensure that we will be okay at the end of the day.

The storm of restlessness passes when we stop and realize that the same Jesus who calmed His disciples is the Jesus who abides with us. He remains in control. The same Jesus who told His disciples, "Your heart must not be troubled. Believe in God; believe also in Me" (John 14:1 HCSB), whispers the same words to us as we face the restless storms of life. Our trust grows when we remember that He handles all that we cannot. He's here, and peace floods the soul in His presence. He's able, and He gives rest to those who have been restless far too long.

Storm Preparation

- What causes restlessness in your life most often?

- How do uncontrollable situations overtake various areas in your life?

- Why does the presence of the Lord bring you peace?

16

AN EXHAUSTING STORM

"David said to himself, 'One of these days, I'll be swept away by Saul. There is nothing better for me than to escape immediately to the land of the Philistines. Then, Saul will stop searching for me everywhere in Israel, and I'll escape from him.'" *1 Samuel 27:1 (HCSB)*

a weariness comes when the storm fails to give a break. Day after day, a threat looms and the body, as well as the mind, begins to struggle as one tries to stay on guard.

In 1971, a system grew to hurricane strength and set a record for most days classified as a hurricane. Hurricane Ginger maintained the status for over twenty-seven consecutive days. The tracking and forecasting of the storm covered an even longer span of time, and the bizarre track of the storm made the system exhausting to follow.

By the time it made landfall near Morehead City, North Carolina, the storm was a minimal hurricane. Much of the damage incurred was to crops in North

Carolina. The storm, however, lives on in history as it circled the Atlantic, drawing close to Bermuda, before turning toward the US mainland. The initial track seemed to indicate it going out to sea, but Ginger's final jaunt collided with the Eastern Seaboard.

Life features times of sheer exhaustion. We find ourselves worn out as storms linger on. What begins as an aggravation drains us over time as it lurks around, day after day, demanding at least a portion of our attention until it finally dissipates.

David knew the storm of exhaustion in his life. After slaying Goliath, and while receiving the praise of the people, he drew the ire of King Saul. Saul set his sights on eliminating the threat, pursuing David relentlessly. David had his chances to kill Saul himself but chose not to take the life of the king. Saul backed off for a moment, then resumed the pursuit, trying to wipe the future king off the face of the earth. Saul's jealousy led to David's exhaustion. By the time we read 1 Samuel 27, you can feel David's pure fatigue.

Eventually, Saul perished, and David ascended to the throne. A new season began where he was no longer on the run. And even in his time of trial, the storm that wore him down, the Lord sustained His servant.

Life wears us out at times. The weight of the storms we face drains us physically so that its damage leaves us empty and desperate for relief. The constant demand to withstand weakens our resolve. Long days and even longer, sleepless nights drag us to a place where we cannot imagine enduring another day, let alone another week. But the Lord steps in when we are too exhausted to take the next breath. He knows our needs, and He knows the details of the situation.

Isaiah 40:31 (CSB) reminds us, "but those who trust in the Lord will renew their strength." You may be exhausted and the thought of the storm continuing to rage robs you of the last ounces of strength in your tank, but God is not tired. He will get you through this storm. Just as He helped David, He will help you soar in a new season. He is the Source of our strength in a time of exhaustion. All we need do is to put our trust in the Lord and be strengthened by His faithfulness. He remains the strength for the weak, the refuge for the worn out.

Storm Preparation

- What storm of life served as the most exhausting in your experience?

- How did you get through that storm and in looking back, how do you see the Lord's hand helping you through that storm?

- What can we do to overcome exhaustion?

A SURPRISE STORM

"When he was told, 'Elisha is in Dothan,' he sent horses, chariots, and
a massive army there. They went by night and surrounded the city."
2 Kings 6:13–14 (CSB)

*n*ot all surprises are good. In fact, there are times when a surprise can be downright terrifying.

A tropical depression grew to a Category 1 storm in less than fifteen hours. Less than two hours after the storm intensified, Hurricane Humberto struck land, packing winds of 80 mph.

The 2007 storm surprised many as it intensified and struck under the cloak of night. The concern earlier in the evening was the slow speed of the system. The intensity startled the unprepared, shook the uninformed. Like a thief in the night, the storm stole the peace of those who thought the system would remain a small depression. What was once just a blip on the radar forced sleepy residents to take note.

What do you do when it comes without warning? How do you react to conditions that deteriorate almost instantly? A surprise storm such as Humberto forces us to hold tight and ride it out because there is nowhere else to run.

Elisha and his servant awoke to a surprise storm. The king of Aram sought to catch Elisha off-guard. He sent a force to surround the man of God at night, so when the next day shed its first light, Elisha and his servant had no way to escape. Though being surrounded by an entire army served as a grim wake-up call, especially for the servant, a God-sized surprise came a few minutes later.

As he scanned the horizon that morning, he saw the obstacle. He rushed back to Elisha and asked, "What are we going to do?"

Elisha prayed. He didn't panic. He refused to devise some quick plan of his own. He prayed. Elisha's prayer asked that the servant's eyes be opened to see. The servant, through the power of the Lord, opened his eyes to see an angel army standing at the ready to help them against the adversary encircling them.

The shock came when the once unseen became visible. The army of man no longer looked too big to overcome when the angel army came into view. Though the servant and Elisha were caught by surprise that morning, the Lord was not.

Life catches us by surprise. Situations arise and struggles emerge without warning. We never planned on facing those sudden storms. A small disturbance in our lives becomes a fierce hurricane. Caught off-guard, we ask like Elisha's servant, "What are we going to do?" Yet, the Lord stands ready, unshaken by that which has shaken us. Instead of focusing on our limited abilities and the lack of a way out, we are prompted to open our eyes to a limitless God.

Instead of listing all those things we cannot do, we say, "What can God do in this storm I'm facing?" He is already at work on it. He was aware of it before the first gust of wind or the first drop of rain. He saw the storm before it struck our lives seemingly from out of nowhere. And He is not shaken. Because of His nature, we can proclaim as David did in Psalm 62, "He alone is my rock and my salvation, my stronghold; I will never be shaken." (Psalm 62:2 CSB)

Storm Preparation

- How do you respond to the surprise storms in life?
- When reading of Elisha and his servant, how can that shift your focus when a storm pops up?
- Why should we remember that we serve a limitless God when the storms rage?

AN EMOTIONAL
STORM

"'Sir,' the sick man answered, 'I don't have a man to put me into the pool when the water is stirred up, but while I'm coming, someone goes down ahead of me.'" *John 5:7 (HCSB)*

*T*he ups and downs of life mirror a ride on a rollercoaster. From the various stages of a storm, the same truth exists. From its approach, to landfall, to the aftermath, hurricanes subject residents to a rollercoaster of emotions.

Hurricane Isabel roared towards the Outer Banks of North Carolina in 2003. The Category 5 storm weakened to a strong Category 2 before striking near Cape Lookout.

The islands took a brutal blow from the rain, winds, flooding, and a severe beating from the storm surge. The storm took an emotional toll on those who call those islands home. As Isabel ate away at the coast, the look of Hatteras Island was transformed. A new inlet formed, spanning an incredible 2,000 feet.

What residents awoke to that day didn't look the same as it had before. The new landscape reminded people of the depth of the storm's fury. To add to the emotional costs, Hatteras Island was cut off from access by road for nearly two months. Nothing remained as it was prior to Isabel's barreling through the area.

For some time, residents of the island grappled with their new situation. Things had changed. Struggles ensued. The very terrain reminded them of a massive strike, long after the strike occurred.

Seasons arise when our emotions feel like a brewing storm. Whether its origins are in the death of a loved one, sickness, disappointments, or other disturbances of life, we face emotional storms in life, and each one is dangerous. The highs and lows remind us of a story that took place by the pool of Bethesda.

A man sat by the pool for a long time, hoping to get into it when the angel stirred the waters up. The first in the pool after the angel's visit found the healing they longed to experience. Without the assistance he needed, this particular man always lost to someone else. As he sat there one day, he found himself again in the emotional storm. He longed to see the waters move but knew he had little chance to get there in time even if they were stirred up.

Yet, there stood Jesus. He asked the man if he wanted to be healed. The despondence of the man, as he shared his struggles, told Jesus of the emotional toll he'd paid over the years. He laid so close, yet still could not immerse himself in time. But, with a few words from Jesus, his hopes materialized. Jesus came and stood in the midst of the sick, and He healed the one others forsook.

Our feelings can range in life from very high to abysmally low. Certain seasons present storms that are all-out assaults on our emotions. We can give up or we can hold on. In the middle of those emotional times, there stands Jesus. He comes to where we are to do what we cannot do on our own. As Psalm 34 puts it, "The Lord is near the brokenhearted; He saves those crushed in spirit." (Psalm 34:18 CSB)

Despondence gives way to dedication in recognition of His presence. Outcasts become the welcomed when Jesus draws near. He causes the regret to give way to rejoicing, and He takes the burden replacing it with a blessing.

Storm Preparation

- What do you do to keep your emotions in check?
- Why does the presence of the Lord immediately help us in an emotional storm?
- What can you do to further embrace His presence and power today?

A PHYSICAL
STORM

"From now on, let no one cause me trouble, because I bear on my body scars for the cause of Jesus." *Galatians 6:17 (HCSB)*

*t*he name Agnes conjures up images of mass destruction to those in the Mid-Atlantic who were alive in 1972. This Gulf hurricane struck the Florida Panhandle and weakened to a tropical depression as it passed through Georgia. However, it regained tropical storm strength when it moved out to sea again off Virginia. It then tore north along the Atlantic states making land-fall on Long Island, New York on its way to Canada. Pennsylvania was especially hard hit by flooding.

Torrential rains devastated the region and destroyed lives, homes, and businesses. Over one hundred people lost their lives in the path of the storm. Estimates as high as 45,000 structures sustained damage. Railroad companies suffered crippling damage and EL Railway filed for bankruptcy later as a result of the storm's impact.

The storm left a physical mark on so many lives and the region. Images of caskets floating up and open left scars on those who saw a reality no one dreamed could happen. What could not be unseen stayed fresh in the minds of those in the path of the storm creating wounds that healed over time but never truly went away completely.

Storms in life leave a mark. Sometimes it is the physical scar that draws our minds back to the day when a storm struck our lives. Those marks remind us of all that happened along the way to get where we are in life. Each stands out; each one reminds us of the difficult nature of life.

Paul knew the struggles of life, especially after meeting Christ on the road to Damascus. He endured shipwrecks and shackles. Opponents issued threats against him. And as he wrote to the Galatians, his body bore the marks. He points to the evidence of the faith in his life, a faith so present it endured physical hardship.

The scars drowned out the voices of those who spoke against him. Each mark focused back to a time he took a stand and paid the price for the sake of Christ. A scar reminds one that they were able to make it through a storm, but the storm left a mark in the process of its passing.

Physical storms rise in all our lives. Scars result. Some of the scars are visible, as were Paul's, and some are hidden within. But the reminders of the wounds are there. Life storms alter the landscape of our lives. The sleepless nights show in our eyes. The outward scars speak to the hurts accumulated over the seasons.

The scars remind us of a truth—God's ability to bring us through the storm. For Paul, the scars were reminders that his faith produced so much evidence that there was something to persecute. Do we have scars for the cause of Christ? Can we look back to see where we've been in the battle for the Lord, or have we simply sat on the sidelines? A physical storm leaves its mark, but when looked at through another lens, the mark speaks louder of God's faithfulness than it does of a storm's forcefulness.

Of all the scars, the ones on the hands and feet of Jesus teach us such an important message. Thomas doubted the resurrection of Christ, but Jesus appeared and invited Thomas to touch the scars. Jesus said, "Put your finger here and observe My hands. Reach out your hand and put it into My side. Don't be an unbeliever, but a believer." (John 20:27 HCSB) Those scars, the physical storm He endured on the cross, remind us that even in the worst physical storms, the Lord will overcome.

Storm Preparation

- What evidence is there in your life that you have suffered for the cause of Christ?

- How do scars in life and faith prove God's faithfulness to us?

- How did Paul's scars help his credibility as a leader for Christ?

A NEAR MISS STORM

"After many days had passed, the Jews conspired to kill him, but their plot became known to Saul. So they were watching the gates day and night intending to kill him, but his disciples took him by night and lowered him in a large basket through an opening in the wall."

Acts 9:23–25 (HCSB)

a prayer to be spared rises from those in the path of destruction.

A system churned in the Atlantic, at one point growing to a Category 4 storm. Edouard (1996) threatened the Eastern Seaboard of the United States. One major problem emerged as no one knew where it would hit. To cover any possible strike, watches and warnings went out from North Carolina to Maine.

The storm passed far enough away from North and South Carolina to minimize the effects. The area around Cape Cod stood in the path. Thankfully, the storm moved just past Nantucket, remaining ninety-five miles offshore.

Though damage came because of the winds and the rains, the area took less of a blow than if a hurricane had made a direct hit.

A near-miss storm should always open our eyes. When a system barrels in our direction, only to turn at the last minute, we have two responses. The first is to praise the Lord for His protection over us. Second, we live with eyes wide open from that moment forward.

Saul met the Lord on the road to Damascus. After the direction of his life changed when Christ called him to live for more, his former allies turned on him. Saul, once the persecutor, became the persecuted. The Jews plotted to kill him, and Saul's only hope was to escape at night. If you look at the Bible's account, the gates were being watched carefully day and night. They were set against any escape by Saul. But here is where God moved. With a slight opening in the wall, Saul was able to escape and God's story through him continued to unfold.

Again, God made a way. Under the cover of night, an escape route appeared. This threat, the storm rising against the Lord's newest leader, closed in more by the minute and just in the nick of time, Saul got away. The Lord performed another perfectly timed escape for Peter when he was in prison. Acts says, "After they passed the first and second guard posts, they came to the iron gate that leads into the city, which opened to them by itself. They went outside and passed one street, and immediately the angel left him." (Acts 12:10 HCSB) What makes the rescue of Peter from prison so amazing was that, if you read Acts 12:6, you understand that the next day, Peter was to be executed. But God showed up. The storms were near misses for these men of God, but the story became about the power and timing of God to make a way.

Many of us can look back at the storms of our lives and see those that turned away at the last minute. We saw God's ability to shift the tides, alter the elements, and preserve us instead of allowing us to be swallowed up in the storm. As storms approach in life, ramp up the prayers. Look back at the near misses in the past. Praise him for His hands being at work.

Don't let a near-miss fail to open your eyes to what could come in the future. Refuse to ignore what could be learned from a close call and ensure you praise Him for the protection only He can provide.

Storm Preparation

- Name a near-miss storm in your life—a life storm that threatened you but never fully struck your life.

- What did you learn from that storm?

- Why do the stories of Saul's escape and Peter's escape from prison give us hope as the storms of life approach?

A STORM
of LONELINESS

"Then He said to them, 'My soul is swallowed up in sorrow—to the point of death. Remain here and stay awake.' Then He went a little farther, fell to the ground, and began to pray that if it were possible, the hour might pass from Him." *Mark 14:34–35 (HCSB)*

What do you do when it feels like there is no one? How do we survive when we feel completely alone?

We take for granted the access we normally have to various people and places. On a normal day, we can freely travel to see others. We traverse with minimal obstructions. Being cut off stands as a nightmare rarely envisioned.

Hurricane Maria (2017) hit the Virgin Islands and Puerto Rico with a vengeance. Puerto Rico and Dominica took some of the worst that Maria had to offer. Thousands died and nearly all the buildings and homes had structural damage. The islands, by nature alone, were separated from other parts of the world, but the hurricane further isolated the residents. Damage to the roadways and bridges kept large portions of roads impassable more than a month after the storm struck the islands.

One storm. In a matter of hours. People were separated from one another, not just those on the mainland, but even those on the same island for over a month. Survivors reeled in the distance between themselves and those who perished in the storm which could not be overcome. Loneliness marked the lives of those who were completely cut off from the life they knew prior to the storm.

No matter who we are, we've endured storms of loneliness. Just as the people on the island of Puerto Rico were distanced from one another, we seem distanced from everyone else at times. The flood of loneliness leaves us drowning in a sea of solitude. Feeling alone isn't a choice but is the aftermath of a direct hit on our lives.

Jesus endured a storm of loneliness. In the Garden of Gethsemane, one of His closest followers committed a horrendous act of betrayal. Upon seeing Him arrested, the eleven others ran as fast and as hard as they could to preserve their own lives. Crowds screamed for Him to die. Soldiers mocked Him. But the depth of His loneliness came a few hours later.

So difficult was the time on the cross that Jesus cried out. Matthew recorded it this way: "About three in the afternoon Jesus cried out with a loud voice, 'Eli, Eli, lema sabachthani?' that is 'My God, My God, why have You forsaken Me?' (Matthew 27:46 HCSB) His lonely cry echoes throughout time and reminds each of us of times we've faced in our personal lives. No one spoke up for Him, but plenty spoke out against Him. And He hung there alone, the weight of isolation evidenced by His words.

Loneliness does not discriminate. Man or woman, old or young, popular or completely overlooked, we all endure the storms of loneliness. When a storm of loneliness strikes, even in a gathering of many souls, we feel isolated. These disturbances leave in their wake feelings of being unloved and having no value. Thoughts of irrelevance cast shadows of doubt on all we set out to accomplish. Drowning in solitary anguish, we long for someone to toss us a lifeline.

Here is the lifeline—Hebrews 13:5 (ESV) says, "I will never leave you nor forsake you." Because of the Lord's presence, you are never alone. Even in a storm that says you are, His Word assures us that He is there. He reaches out to you as your life preserver and reminds you that even if no one else in the world seems to want you, He will never stop wanting you.

Storm Preparation

- When in your life has a storm of loneliness struck you?

- How does Jesus' experience in the garden and on the cross help you as you face loneliness in your life?

- How can Hebrews 13:5 give us strength even when we are enduring a storm of loneliness in our lives?

A STORM
of REGRET

"Then Judas, His betrayer, seeing that he had been condemned, was
full of remorse and returned the thirty pieces of silver to the chief
priests and elders." *Matthew 27:3 (HCSB)*

What crossed south Florida as a Tropical Depression sat in the Gulf of
Mexico and moved around erratically. As this hurricane approached
the Gulf Coast, the storm slowed and intensified. Overnight, just before landfall in Alabama, Sally (2020) grew to a strong Category 2.

What stood out was the destruction left behind by the increased furor of
the storm. Many failed to anticipate such a powerful storm. In the aftermath,
some officials vocalized their misgivings.

The mayor of Gulf Shores expressed his regret in an interview after Sally
moved away. Like many others, he believed the storm would be more of a
nuisance than a nightmare. Robert Craft mentioned that the storm, "suck-
er-punched us" and that "no one took it as seriously, including me, as we

should have." Even the National Weather Service failed to fully anticipate the massive hit the town would experience when Sally came ashore.

What followed Hurricane Sally was a storm of regret. Though dealing with a hurricane is anything but guaranteed, some wished they had erred on the side of caution more than they did. As they looked back, they saw what could have been done had they taken the threat more seriously.

We live much of our lives looking back. The storms of regret howl when mistakes haunt our memories and the price of our actions fully plays out.

Judas sold out Jesus. For thirty pieces of silver, he turned his back on Christ and betrayed Him with a kiss. As the follower turned foe watched what they did to Jesus, he regretted what he had done but what was done was done. Nothing was going to change the course of the events that unfolded after Judas' betrayal. He tried to return the money and his regret led to Judas taking his own life. He could not live with what he had done.

Regret often swarms our minds in life. The enemy reminds us of every shortcoming. He whispers, 'You failed.' He strives to convince us that we can never overcome our past, and there is no hope for our future. We pass by that place where we did something regrettable in the past. At the grocery store, we see someone we hurt, and the flashes of what happened fill the mind. Regret robs you of what God wants to do through your life today.

Are you enduring a storm of regret? Does your past feel like it's too much to overcome? There is a calm that comes in this storm. No matter who you are or what you've done, the cross offers you a new start, calm from the punishing winds of the past and waves of remorse. The Bible promises us that all those mistakes, when repented of and confessed, are removed from us.

Allow the Lord to calm the storm within you today. Trust that He is faithful to forgive just as the Word promised us. John wrote, "If we confess our sins, He is faithful and righteous to forgive us our sins and cleanse us from all unrighteousness." (1 John 1:9 HCSB) Give God a chance to show us how He can use our past and His power to help someone else in the future. Open your ears to hear Him say, 'Forgiven.'

Storm Preparation

- How do the regrets of your past paralyze you in a storm of regret?

- Why does the enemy try to force us to focus on our failures?

- How does the forgiveness of God calm a storm of regret?

A STORM *of* HOPELESSNESS

"But He was in the stern, sleeping on the cushion. So, they woke Him up and said to Him, 'Teacher! Don't You care that we're going to die?'" *Mark 4:38 (CSB)*

*i*f the seas threaten to swallow us, where does our hope lie in those moments?

Every storm leaves a story in its wake. Though the elements change as the storm passes, the unsettled transition to a more settled atmosphere, lingering from the days it churned ashore, extends beyond its exit. Hurricane Joaquin's (2015) story reminds us all of the strength of a storm and the hopelessness that can envelop a soul.

The storm battered the Bahamas, but it is the story of a battered ship that echoes still today. The El Faro, a cargo ship, found itself in the worst of Joaquin's fury on the open sea. She was taking on water, and unable to reach dry land. A frantic crew tried to maintain control of the vessel, but the storm was too much to overcome. They decided to evacuate but, even as they did, one of the crew cried out, "I'm a goner!"

The hopelessness of the statement tears at the heart. The storm was simply too much. With the weight of nature bearing down, the man cried out as life crumbled in the maelstrom. The wrath of the sea promised no way out and, sadly, the entire crew of the El Faro perished on October 1, 2015. Thirty-three members of the crew lost their lives and the despair of the one vocalized the terror of a situation turned hopeless.

Hopelessness rocks a life just as waves rock a ship. Tossing everything from side to side, the storm shifts our reality. "Am I going down?" becomes a question not of if it will happen, or if one will be overtaken, but when.

The disciples endured moments of hopelessness on the open waters. A storm struck in an area known for quick developing storms. Once peaceful waters angrily attacked their vessel, threatening to overturn the boat and its passengers. They fought an uncertain fate. As water poured in, they worked feverishly to bail it out. As the boat rocked, they worked to stabilize it. Twelve men fought the elements, to the point of feeling hopeless about their chances of survival.

Exhausted physically, frantic mentally, they rushed inside to find Jesus asleep. "Don't You care that we are going to die?" they cried out. The situation said there was no hope, but Hope was riding in the boat that day. In the face of certain death, their cries reached the ears of the Author of life. And He moved. He rose and emerged from the inside of the ship. He called out three words, "Peace! Be still!" and the storm was no more.

Astonishment replaced their earlier hopelessness. How could He calm such a raging storm? Hope overcame and their eyes were opened to His power to calm the seas. When Hope spoke, hopelessness lost its grip on the lives of twelve men.

Nothing stands as truly hopeless before the Lord. He is our hope. As the psalmist writes, "But I will hope continually and will praise You more and more." (Psalm 71:14 CSB) When storms of hopelessness rage, He is stirred by the cries of those He loves. Are we crying out to others about our situation, or do we cry out to the Savior who can change the situation? If Christ is truly our hope, as He is to be, the raging storm inside us subsides with just a few words from Him.

Storm Preparation

- How do you identify with the situation the disciples faced on the sea?

- Why is our prayer life of utmost importance when life seems to be hopeless?

- How has Jesus given you hope in the past and how can that help you when you face storms of hopelessness in the future?

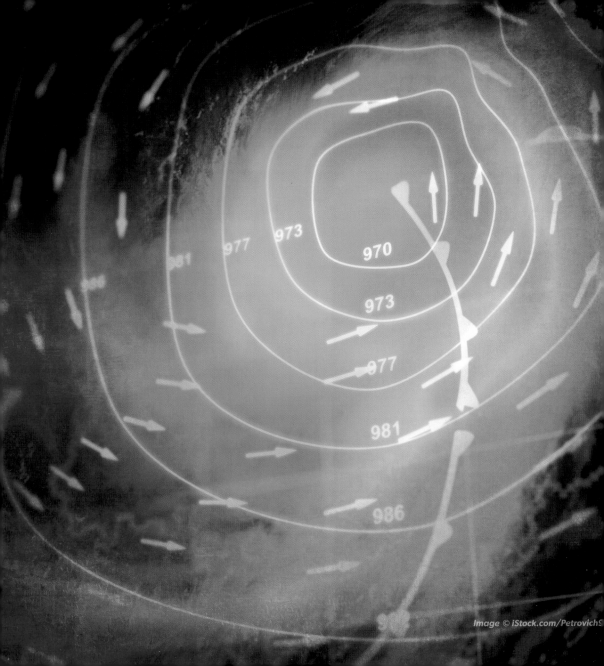

AN ANTICIPATED STORM

"I have told you these things so that in Me you may have peace. You will have suffering in this world. Be courageous! I have conquered the world." *John 16:33 (CSB)*

*a*ny warning is better than no warning at all. Storms have existed since Genesis 6 and, over time, we've gotten better at tracking, forecasting, predicting, and warning of a storm's arrival. The desire to preserve the lives of as many as possible led to new methods, with an increased attention on conditions turning deadly.

In 1875, hurricane flags were implemented to warn the public that a storm loomed. The flags featured a red background with a black square in the middle. At night, the flags were illuminated to ensure the warning was visible to all, at all times. Long before television, these warnings towered above the community in an attempt to alert an unsuspecting public. Any advance warning could mean life or death, and better preparation versus no preparation at all.

Now, we can see storms with even earlier warning. Forecasts of their development begin while they are still thousands of miles away. But even in the 1800s, the desperate goal existed to alert the public to dangerous conditions. The desire to help others survive pushed leaders to design ways to make known a coming storm.

As Jesus's time drew closer, the cross came more into focus. He knew what His closest followers didn't understand—He knew a storm was coming. Because of His great love for them, He tried to prepare them. What He said to them provided them with the opportunity to get ready, even if they questioned what to expect. Any preparation was better than no preparation at all.

He foretold of struggles and suffering. He warned of rejection and persecution. With the warning in John 16, He issued a final statement as the storm made its approach. Landfall of the storm, headed by the chief priests and Pharisees, loomed as Jesus and the disciples made their way to the Garden of Gethsemane.

The storm raged. Threats against their lives continued until the Lord called them home. By the guidance of the Lord, the truth of the words Jesus spoke raised the awareness of His followers. Eyes opened to the dangers, took note of the changing conditions, and saw the real nature of the wolves parading around in sheep's clothing.

A storm anticipated becomes a storm more easily endured. When there is a forewarning, we can prepare ahead of time, strengthen what is standing, and find refuge before the storm strikes. Jesus assured His followers that they would face struggles and suffering. He pointed to the fact that the world hated Him and would naturally hate His followers too.

He continued, "Remember the word I spoke to you: 'A slave is not greater than his master.' If they persecuted Me, they will also persecute you. If they kept My word, they will also keep yours." (John 15:20 HCSB)

Know that storms will come. Be aware that conditions can change at any moment. Jesus hoisted the warning flags before the cross—now we must heed the warnings ourselves. By committing the Word of God to our hearts, we can withstand the worst of the storm.

Storm Preparation

- Why does an advance warning help you prepare for a storm that is approaching?

- Why do you believe Jesus warned the disciples ahead of time?

- How do His warnings help us live our lives better and more aware today?

STORMS
of ANXIETY

"Don't worry about anything, but in everything, through prayer and petition with thanksgiving, let your requests be made known to God." *Philippians 4:6 (HCSB)*

*W*e could relax if only we knew what was coming. If we knew the outcome, we could find peace.

Major hurricanes draw the eyes and the attention of those thought to be in the path of the storm. In 1999, a major hurricane formed in the Gulf of Mexico. Hurricane Bret exploded into a Category 4 storm as it turned towards the coast of Texas. Where would it strike? How strong would the storm be at landfall?

Bret's approach led to anxious times in the lives of those on the shores of the Lone Star State. A decade had passed since Texas took a direct hit from a storm at hurricane strength. Bret's path promised a landfall and, as the hours ticked away, tensions rose.

Nearly 200,000 coastal residents evacuated. The storm made landfall, but where it came ashore was less populated than other areas of Texas. The storm further weakened and completely dissipated, relieving the tensions of many who feared catastrophic damage from the storm. Of all the scenarios, outside of the storm completely falling apart before making landfall in Texas, the path Bret took was one of the best possible outcomes.

Anxiety brews as storms develop in our world. The primary focus is what will be the result from the system. Will I be able to make it? Will I survive? How will my life be if the storm hits me? With each question, the storm of anxiety rages even more.

As Jesus spoke to a crowd gathered on a hillside, He understood their lives. More than they understood themselves, He knew them. Christ saw the look in their eyes and spoke to the worries of their hearts. His guidance offered them a new way to live. He told them, "Don't worry."

Jesus knew that anxiety stole the focus of a life and robbed each of hope. The presence of those anxieties ate away at the abundant life He came to give. His teaching in the Sermon on the Mount was to live a life of righteousness and allow God to handle the worries of the day. He instructed, "But seek first the kingdom of God and His righteousness, and all these things will be provided for you." (Matthew 6:33 CSB) To paraphrase—do what God calls you to do and trust He will do what He said He will do. Paul, in his letter to the Philippians, also alluded to the cure for a storm of anxiety. Turn to God, let go of the uncontrollable, and praise Him for being in control.

Storms of apprehension strike every person, no matter what makes up their life story. Rich and poor, young and old, all face the unsettling in this life. As those squalls approach, we can be overcome by the storm, or we can follow what Jesus said and listen to what Paul instructed. By seeking the kingdom first, we reach towards the Lord with all that we have in the understanding that He is faithful to all who are faithful to Him.

Rather than fixate on the uncontrollable, let's handle what we can control—chasing after Jesus. That anxiety of "worst-case scenario" dissipates when we trust the One who can handle the outcome.

Storm Preparation

- What in life causes you the greatest anxiety on a daily basis?

- What verses of Scripture speak out against those anxieties and which verses can strengthen you when storms of anxiety approach?

- Why do you think Jesus wanted to alleviate the anxieties of the crowd and why did Paul want to help the Philippians overcome their anxieties?

Image © iStock.com/andykatz

STORMS *of*
PERSECUTION

"You are blessed when they insult and persecute you and falsely say
every kind of evil against you because of Me. Be glad and rejoice,
because your reward is great in heaven. For that is how they persecuted the prophets who were before you." *Matthew 5:11–12 (CSB)*

a deadly storm tore through the Dominican Republic, Puerto Rico, and
Dominica, proving itself to be one of the deadliest hurricanes on
record. Hurricane David shattered the lives and properties of thousands in
late August/early September of 1979. Two thousand deaths occurred in the
Dominican Republic alone. After trashing the island, the hurricane continued
toward the United States.

Warnings blanketed much of the southeast coast of the United States. When
David's impact on south Florida was less than expected, criticism arose. The
position of those in leadership was to be on the safe side, but the detractors
hurled their criticism rather than offer praise. Instead of their focus being on the

minimal impact of a storm that threatened to wreak havoc, the critics tried to tear down the experts who did their best to keep people safe.

Persecution comes in all forms. Open persecution threatens in action and word. Passive persecution questions motives or belittles the efforts of an individual. For anyone, persecution easily detracts and derails us. We harbor the frustration of the moment, and we tire of giving all we have only to be beaten down. But Jesus said to rejoice! He calls for us to be glad even when persecution comes to us.

His words from Matthew 5 seem illogical at best. How can anyone enjoy ridicule? Who enjoys the insults of others or the pressure of persecution on a daily basis? Why did He say that those who endure such treatment were blessed? Yet Jesus gives us insight. He says that we should rejoice because of the origin of the persecution—it comes because of His name. To be ridiculed or even outcast for the name of Jesus is to be identified as a follower of Jesus! Those who are persecuted for their faith exhibit enough faith in their lives to invite oppression. Those of little faith give little reason for any opposition to come their way.

Secondly, Jesus told them to rejoice because their reward in heaven was great. Persecution, even a storm of persecution in your life, lasts for only a fixed amount of time. Persecutors move on to the next person they want to beat down. Those creating trouble for you eventually find themselves being held accountable by God. The insults silence when they lose their effectiveness. But while that is fixed on a timeline, rewards in heaven are forever. Those rewards never end and never diminish in value.

When a storm of persecution strikes, remind yourself that Jesus said it will be worth it. They persecuted Him and they will naturally persecute us too. Rejoice that they see Jesus in you. Be glad that the storm will pass but your reward in heaven will not.

Storm Preparation

- How do Jesus' words in Matthew 5 help us when we are in the middle of a storm of persecution?

- What can rejoicing in persecution do to your overall outlook?

- What can you do to stand firm in the face of a storm of persecution?

AN UPENDING STORM

> "'Who are You, Lord?' he said. 'I am Jesus, the One you are persecuting,' He replied. 'But get up and go into the city, and you will be told what you must do.'" *Acts 9:5–6 (HSCB)*

a major Category 5 hurricane promised to turn the islands upside down. Hurricane Irma wreaked havoc in the Caribbean and Saint Martin, as well as St. Barthelemy, took a direct hit. The normal laid-back nature of island living became an overwhelming quest to stay alive.

September 6, 2017 is a day that stands out to those on the islands. A vegetative land stood bare and exposed as the monster system bore down, stripping away the beauty on display just forty-eight hours earlier. An entire way of life tossed upside down as the storm tore away what was and forced people to face something altogether new. Villages that once dotted the islands were relegated to mere memories. Entire industries failed to endure the storm's wrath.

For survivors of Irma, the 2017 storm upended their lives, their hopes, and their dreams. What remained was the opportunity to make a new start and build a new life. Though the overhaul was powerful, the fact they had a new day was promising. Life stood in the balance in the storm; to have survived it meant there was a second chance for their lives, even if it meant starting all over.

Some storms of life flip our world upside down. The agony of letting go of what was subsides a little when we see the next day as a gift of mercy, a true opportunity to chart a new path.

Saul believed in his heart that he was doing the right thing in trying to stop the advance of the gospel. Tirelessly, he sought to pursue what he believed to be his purpose. As he traveled the road to Damascus, he intended to expand his power to arrest believers, further silencing the gospel. On the journey, though, Christ upended the life of Saul as the power of man faced the power of God.

A blinding light crippled Saul and took his eyesight. As he called out, the Lord spoke to a new life for Saul. The Lord instructed Saul to go and live that new life, complete with a new purpose. From persecuting to proselytizing, his life flipped upside down on the road. But what really happened? He was given a chance at new life.

Saul took the opportunity and never looked back. He sought to live life according to the One he encountered on the road to Damascus. Days of blindness gave way to new vision. What seemed to be turned upside down was the Lord's way of turning Saul right side up.

Some storms upend our entire existence. They alter every facet of life in such a way that nothing remains the same as it was before. When life gets overhauled, mercy says it's a new beginning. We weren't swept away by the storm, but what was swept away leaves open a door for new life to emerge.

God's grace redirects our entire lives. He holds a better plan than any we design ourselves. In such a storm, one that reorients our lives, we can embrace a new call from Him, live for His glory, and see how He allowed the storm because He called us to more than the life we lived before.

Storm Preparation

- How is a storm that upends your life an act of mercy and grace by God?

- How did Saul's storm change his story and impact others in the long run?

- What can you praise God for today that He has taken away from your life in the past?

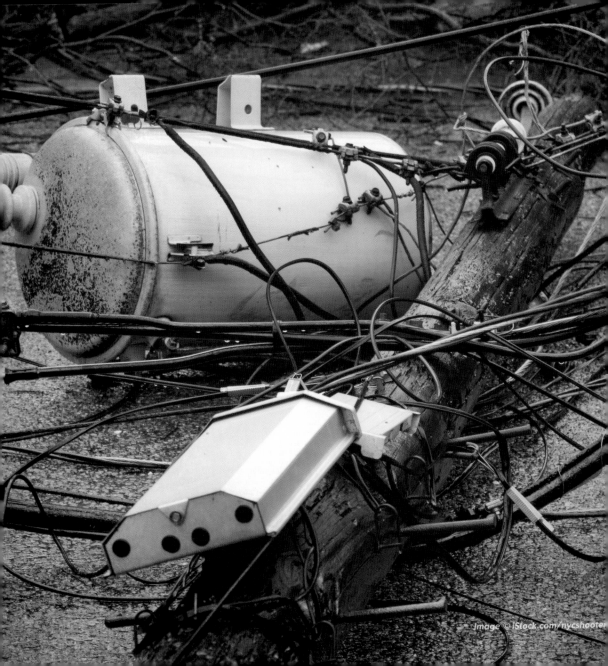

28

AN UNFORGIVING STORM

"'Teacher', they said to Him, 'this woman was caught in the act of committing adultery. In the law Moses commanded us to stone such women. So, what do You say?'" John 8:4–5 (HCSB)

*e*ven a momentary reprieve gave way to a reclaimed intensity. As Hurricane Allen (1980) came through the Gulf of Mexico, the storm reached the highest category for hurricanes on three different occasions. Churning up the waters as a Category 5 storm, Allen lashed out.

Weakened for a moment as it passed through Cuba and Hispaniola, Allen mercilessly grew stronger after the weakening, the winds topping out at an alarming 190 miles per hour. Friction from the land typically slows the tropical systems down, but in the open seas, they strengthen as they feed on warmer waters. Allen's intensity rebuilt unobstructed as it cleared Cuba.

Allen finally made landfall in Texas as a Category 3 storm but what this storm will be remembered for was its unforgiving nature. Allen set records for wind speed in the Atlantic basin and refused to quiet down and go away. Allen blew with all the gusto it could muster and left its mark in the record books.

Life's storms can emerge in different areas of life. There are terrifying storms of guilt. Some are storms directed at our health. Some, however, are storms of unforgiveness, spiraling out of control after we've made a mistake. The weight of the world bears down on us and the pressure intensifies. Clouds darken as we approach those who refuse to forgive. Rumbles of thunder echo in the background as we feel the stares of others. We want that storm to pass but we have no control over its duration.

The scribes and Pharisees longed to cause Jesus to stumble. If He slipped, He would stand discredited in the eyes of the crowds who constantly pressed in to hear more. As they caught a woman in adultery, they believed it was the perfect situation to trap Jesus in front of a crowd.

Her shame put on display for all to see, they humiliated her. She had committed adultery; her sin not in question as she was caught in the act. The religious leaders put her in the center of the crowd and told of her mistake. She needed forgiveness, only a little compassion from others who had not lived perfect lives, but they were unwilling. A storm of unforgiveness swirled around her as they demanded her death. They dragged her personal shame into the light as accusations and condemnation filled the air.

Jesus stooped and wrote in the sand. The mob pressed even more. He kept writing. Finally, He told them that if they were perfect, they could throw the first stone at her. One by one, when faced with their own nature, they walked away, unable to live up to the standard by which they could condemn her. After the crowd cleared, she found the calm in the storm, and in Christ, she received the forgiveness she needed.

Storms of unforgiveness hurt us. The swirling of accusations and the waves of shame threaten to overtake us. Yet when we turn to Jesus, we find the forgiveness we need. He calls us to go forward and sin no more, just as He told the woman that day. He is faithful to forgive even when others are unwilling to offer forgiveness. In the middle of a storm of unforgiveness, Jesus alone calms the storm with His power to forgive on an eternal level. And when we receive that forgiveness, we must freely offer that forgiveness to others who find themselves in such a storm in their lives.

Storm Preparation

- When have you faced unforgiveness and how did it feel to endure that storm?

- Why should we turn to the Lord to ask for His forgiveness first and foremost after we fall short?

- Why should we be forgiving of others?

29

A PAINFUL
STORM

"For our momentary light affliction is producing for us an absolutely incomparable eternal weight of glory." 2 Corinthians 4:17 (HCSB)

a deadly storm swirled in late October and early September of 1998. Hurricane Mitch, a massive Category 5 hurricane brought immense winds and rains to Honduras and other parts of Central America. It triggered mudslides and thrust the affected areas, especially Honduras, into economic turmoil.

More destruction and fallout from Mitch came in the sinking of The Fantome. The lives of all crew members aboard the vessel were lost at sea. The storm overcame the vessel, its force too great for the boat to withstand.

As we look back at Hurricane Mitch, the pain that resulted from the storm stands out. Thousands perished in the storm, from those out on the waters to those swept away in the mudslides and flooding. Families torn apart by death highlight Mitch as one of the most painful storms ever. The storm left behind scars on the hearts of survivors.

Pain leaves marks on various portions of our lives. We remember each event, every word, and the very actions that broke our hearts. In the middle of that storm, we feel the constant sting, but there is a truth in the Bible that helps us to overcome the painful storms of our existence.

Paul wrote to the Corinthians hoping to guide them and encourage them. The believers in Corinth faced many challenges and persecutions. To follow their faith, they had to endure hardships. Affliction promised to be ever-present as they lived counterculture, but Paul made sure they understood the long-term truth.

Pain exists. It hurts. Paul refused to ignore the existence of pain in this life, the hurts of this broken world. The apostle, however, taught the Corinthians to look beyond the momentary struggle and focus on the eternal. He said the afflictions, the agonies of the day, were only momentary. They hurt for a time, but they are not meaningless. They are leading somewhere. Paul wrote that the end game—the eternal weight of glory— is worth the momentary pains of this life. Those very words encouraged the believers to endure the pain, to push through the storm of hardship, by pressing forward toward eternity.

A Psalm touches on the passing storm of pain in life. Psalm 30 says, "Weeping may spend the night, but there is joy in the morning." (Psalm 30:5 HCSB) Pain results from the original sin, the fall of man, but by His grace, we do not endure the pain for nothing. Though today may be a storm of pain like no other, joy will come. The joy of the risen Son reminds us that we can celebrate each rising of the sun.

Pain is a part of this life but it, much like life, is passing. It is only a moment in time. When the storm of pain comes, praise God that there is an eternity devoid of any pain we will enjoy one day in the presence of Jesus!

Storm Preparation

- What brought you the most pain in your life and what helped you to get through that storm?

- How does scripture help us to overcome pain?

- Why was it important for Paul to get the Corinthians to push through the pains of this life?

A MENTAL STORM

"This man came to Him at night and said, 'Rabbi, we know that You have come from God as a teacher, for no one could perform these signs You do unless God were with Him.'" *John 3:2 (HCSB)*

a hurricane memorial stands in Toronto, Canada, memorializing the day in 1954 when the city endured one of its worst natural disasters. Hurricane Hazel, a storm so potent that it nearly wiped Garden City, South Carolina, off the map, held so much force that it impacted life in another country.

Hazel came ashore near Calabash, North Carolina, packing estimated winds of 130 miles per hour. The Category 4 storm decimated the beachfront then moved inland to carry out more destruction. Though extratropical by the time it reached Toronto, the system impacted lives after traveling over 1,000 miles on land. Hazel's memory remains etched in the minds of those who lived through the storm.

Psychology Today published a piece in 2021 about Hurricane Hazel and the effect it had on Toronto. In the piece, Dr. Ilan Kelmar included this observation: "Toronto recovered, burying its dead, weeping with the bereaved, and supporting the rescuers haunted by those they could not save and those who drowned from their own ranks." A mental storm emerged from a hurricane that took Toronto by storm.[1]

Mental storms batter the individual mercilessly. Whether it be the mental trauma of an event or the multitude of questions raging in the mind during this life, a mental storm is nothing short of draining. Is there hope in the mental storms of life? As we wade through what we know, what we think, and what we hope for, we seek a refuge in the mind.

Nicodemus, a Pharisee, found himself locked in a mental storm of his own. Jesus took the region by storm and inevitably, the Pharisees heard the claims made by Jesus and His followers. At the same time, Nicodemus heard what his colleagues said about the Man from Nazareth. The religious leadership dismissed His words and His works in an effort to diminish His effectiveness among the masses. Nicodemus took all the thoughts into account and wrestled with it until he could bear the storm no more. The mental storm of the day left him with but one option.

Under the cloak of night, Nicodemus traveled. He waited until he was least likely to be seen and went to where he heard this Jesus was staying. There, he asked questions and listened intently to the explanations Jesus gave. He went to the Source to find the solutions to calm the storm raging inside. And Jesus provided. We later see Nicodemus at the cross, helping take Jesus' body for burial. He no longer needed to sneak in by night; he was there in broad daylight.

1 Toronto's Actions After Hurricane Hazel Still Reap Rewards | Psychology Today

The mind needs to be clear if we truly want to carry out the Lord's will and know Him. Paul said that it begins by shifting the mind onto the things above and not the things of this earth. That which is heavenly serves as a reminder that the troubles of this world will not exist when this life comes to an end.

So many questions exist. So much turmoil plagues the mind. The assault of a mental storm may threaten our sanity, but never forget, we have a Savior. When answers are hard to come by, we turn to the Answer and allow Him to calm our heart and mind with His truth for our soul. Pray for the peace of mind that only comes for the true Giver of peace, the Lord Jesus Christ.

Storm Preparation

- What causes you a mental storm most often in your life?

- What does Nicodemus teach us about dealing with the questions in our minds?

- How does Jesus help to clear our minds, putting our minds to rest, even in the most vicious storms of our lives?

A HUMBLING STORM

"At the end of 12 months, as he was walking on the roof of the royal palace in Babylon, the king exclaimed, 'Is this not Babylon the Great that I have built by my vast power to be a royal residence and to display my majestic glory?'" Daniel 4:29–30 (HCSB)

*i*n July of 1960, some enjoyed the fruits of their labor and life on an island. Joy in the summer months in Saint Maarten gave way to a drastically different life after Hurricane Donna spun through the region. A wave became a depression, and a depression led to a storm. When Donna reached hurricane strength, it grew and had Sint Maarten in its crosshairs.

Winds of 125 miles per hour battered the island of thirteen square miles. The storm took the stability of before and flattened it in a matter of hours. One of the island paradises of the Caribbean lay in ruins. The power of nature overwhelmed the people. Donna proved to be a humbling storm as reports estimated up to twenty-five percent of the people were homeless in its aftermath.

Life has a way of humbling us. Sometimes it hurls a storm our way to accomplish its goal. Sudden changes in life humble us. At any moment, what was taken for granted a month prior can be taken away a month later. What we believed would stand forever can fall in minutes when a storm descends.

Nebuchadnezzar walked out one day and gazed a little too long on what he believed to be his own creation. The majestic nature of the city intoxicated him to the point that he said aloud, "I have built this by my vast power." A humbling storm came quickly thereafter. So fast was the storm that the Bible says it swept him up before he could finish the statement about his greatness. Into the field he went, stripped of the lavish life he knew moments earlier. He boasted of his great power. He trumpeted his own majestic glory. And just like that, he was removed.

The king inherited a new kingdom. The new one lacked a palace and the meal offerings paled in comparison to his time as king. His new palace was an open field, living among the beasts. For his diet, no longer was there a spread of the finest foods of the day, instead he snacked on the grass of the field. Even his appearance changed drastically. His nails become like the claws of a bird. He lived powerless, lacking any influence, and held none of the majestic glory he boasted of previously.

Just as Nebuchadnezzar needed to be humbled, so do we. A humbling storm is always for our good. When we mistakenly neglect to acknowledge God's greatness and begin to tout our own efforts, we need something to knock us down a bit. When the Lord humbles us, that is a blessing. He chooses to give us another chance to acknowledge His greatness, His power, and live for His glory. Some storms of life are intended to humble us lest we begin to believe we no longer need God.

Humility brings us back to the place of right standing before God. Jesus explained it this way, "For everyone who exalts himself will be humbled, and the one who humbles himself will be exalted." (Luke 14:11 HCSB) God humbles us so that we remain in the right position before Him. As He humbles us, He reveals our need for Him in all things.

Storm Preparation

- How has a storm of life in the past humbled you in a way you needed to be humbled?

- What do you learn from Nebuchadnezzar that you can hold on to for your own good?

- Why does it hurt to be humbled in life?

AN UNCONTROLLABLE STORM

"He lived in the tombs. No one was able to restrain him anymore—even with chains—because he often had been bound with shackles and chains but had snapped off the chains and smashed the shackles. No one was strong enough to subdue him." *Mark 5:3–4 (HCSB)*

*O*phelia grew from a tropical storm to a hurricane only to diminish to tropical storm status. As conditions for growth improved, Ophelia became a hurricane again, Forecasters watched as the storm rose and fell in intensity in September 2005. Some models suggested the storm would cross Florida to enter the Gulf of Mexico. Ophelia, however, decided to move into the Atlantic.

Ophelia weakened and intensified three times, and the hurricane's track baffled many. After appearing to head out to sea, Ophelia meandered around, then made a clockwise turn to circle back towards the Carolinas. Ophelia skirted the shores of the Outer Banks before moving off to the North Sea. A look at Ophelia's track shows the uncontrollable nature of the storm.

Uncontrollable storms terrorize us because we know we have no power over them, and we cannot know with any certainty what it may do. We try to plan out what the storm may bring, how big the destruction may be, and what could be the outcome. But much of life remains out of our control. Storms unleash whatever they choose, and we choose to focus on the uncontrollable or on what we can control.

A man lived in the tombs and because of what lived inside of him; no one wanted to be around him. So out of control was he that they tried to subdue him with shackles and chains. Nothing worked. The demons inside him refused to let him be constrained, so he snapped the chains and continued to terrorize others.

People avoided him at all costs. No one knew what he might do, and they recognized they were powerless to subdue him. Their past time and effort proved that. Then came Jesus. The Lord traveled that way and, for once, the man among the tombs encountered the One who stood in complete control. Jesus called the spirits to come out, setting the man free from the torment he endured so long. The spirits held no power over Jesus. With a few words, He proved His power over that which the world perceived as uncontrollable. And the man, after being delivered, no longer threatened uncontrollably but was transformed immediately.

We struggle with that which is out of our control, but that's when we should turn immediately to Jesus. Out of control storms rage, threatening us with their instability, but in those moments, we turn to our stability,

Jesus Christ, and trust that He is still in control. His consistency calms our souls when we face uncertainty. He brings about order from chaos and He reveals His power and control when life feels completely unhinged.

By turning over control of our life to Him, we free ourselves to live more of the life we are called to live. We then step out in faith and allow the Lord to dictate the outcome. Storms still rage but His strength becomes our focus even in the most unpredictable circumstance.

Storm Preparation

- What out of control storm of life is most memorable to you in your past?

- How does remembering that Jesus is ultimately in control help you when you face the uncontrollable in life?

- What verses about the Lord being in control help you as you face those elements of life that are out of your control?

LEARNING FROM *the* STORMS OTHERS ENDURE

"Now faith is the reality of what is hoped for, the proof of what is not seen.
For our ancestors won God's approval by it." *Hebrews 11:1–2 (HCSB)*

*t*hose who fail to learn from the happenings of the past are destined to experience hardships that could have been avoided. Though each hurricane is unique unto itself, some similarities exist. From each system experienced, improvements can be made, whether it be on the forecasting side or the preparation side of the equation.

Hurricane Katrina rocked Louisiana in 2005. The storm devastated New Orleans and surrounding areas, shattering lives, and leaving behind a multitude of questions with few answers. The world continued to turn, more storms came and went, but outside of Louisiana, life went on with little pause.

Georgia Institute of Technology, however, took the time to reflect. Though the university is located in Atlanta, researchers sought to uncover what could be learned from the tragedy. Why put forth the effort? Researchers believed that lessons could be learned to save lives and minimize damage from future storms. The researchers learned that the buildings built to withstand wind succumbed to the storm surge. With issues like climate change, the researchers suggested that understanding such changes could help avoid massive loss of life in the future.

The truly wise learn from the world around them. One generation learns from the errors of previous generations to avoid repeating their mistakes. Those who study the world around them see the pitfalls others fall into and take precautions to avoid the same holes. From the storms of others, we learn *if* we keep our eyes and ears open.

The Bible has an entire chapter that instructs the reader to learn from the faith of others who walked this earth long before the letter was written. The stories in the chapter incredibly detail the heroes of the faith and what the Lord can do through faith. But if you look a little closer, there are proclamations for how people of faith overcame storms of life through faith and the power of God.

One overcame a flood, and another overcame the storm of oppression and being trapped by the Red Sea. Faith conquered. As the chapter progresses, the writer of Hebrews points out tales of the lions' den, shackles being broken, gaining strength when weak, and so many others. These

Bible heroes learned, just as we do, from their faith. And we can learn from the storms they faced.

God teaches us. From the storms of those in the Bible to the storms churning in the world around us, we learn from faith, and we learn from mistakes. Hebrews 11 spoke of giant faith and its ability to endure even the greatest storms that strike our lives. From what we learn and what we experience, we pass the knowledge on to the next generation.

The Word provides us with examples and insights. Storms will come, but most of these storms have come before in some form. Taking the time to study what others have endured is never a waste of effort. If anything, it prepares us, should a similar storm arise. Knowing that we can prepare for the storms to come and be ready to stand when they strike.

Storm Preparation

- How do the experiences of others help you as you face storms in your life?

- Faith triumphs are listed in Hebrews 11. How do those triumphs strengthen you for what you may face in life this week?

- How can you use the storms you've faced in your life to help someone else better prepare for or endure the storms they face?

STORMS
that HAVE
WIDESPREAD
REACH

"Saul, however, was ravaging the church. He would enter house after house, drag off men and women, and put them in prison." *Acts 8:3 (HCSB)*

*h*urricane Georges assured its name would go down in history. A product of the 1998 Atlantic Hurricane season, Georges grew to major hurricane strength, topping out at 155 miles per hour sustained wind speed. What makes Georges even more memorable was a different factor.

So many felt the force of Hurricane Georges. In total, the late September hurricane struck people in the islands and the United States. Seven landfalls showed the ability of a storm to affect the lives of people thousands of miles apart. Antigua took a direct hit, as did St. Kitts a mere three hours later. Puerto Rico could not escape its brutal force.

Key West fell in the storm's path, and Georges made its final strike on the shores of Biloxi, Mississippi. Many felt the impact of this storm that set its sights on destruction. Georges claimed many lives, destroyed properties, and left behind widespread devastation.

So often, we face personal storms in life, ones that seem to only affect us as an individual. There are many, however, that affect lives in other places as well. Recessions and depressions in the economy affect people across the nation. Drought and hurricanes affect entire regions and touch many lives. Persecution also has a way of impacting multiple people.

Saul set in motion a storm of persecution. His desire was to stop the movement of the gospel. By throwing people in prison and spreading fear throughout the region, Saul impacted many lives through his wrath. Families were torn apart, and gatherings of believers dispersed as their adversary threatened the lives of any who aligned themselves with the gospel.

So many faced the same storm. From that truth emerges a beauty even in the middle of a desperate struggle. Those facing the storm didn't have to face it alone. Others understood what was happening. Fellow believers felt the same fear and experienced some of the same devastation. As Saul sought to tear at the seams of the gospel movement, he could not tear away what truly held them together—their bond in Christ.

Storms of life often isolate. We imagine that no one else faces the same struggle. But some storms touch multiple lives, and in those storms, we don't have to ride them out alone. We can strengthen one another, encourage each other, and be there to help when others struggle and need a hand. God gives us companionship and relationships with others, so we are never on an island battling the storms of life alone.

Stand in the gap for those going through the same storm as you are facing. Grow together in this time and see that you are not alone in this fight. Share how the Lord helped you and seek encouragement when you feel overwhelmed.

Storm Preparation

- How does it help you to know others are facing what you are going through?

- Why do you believe that God gives us the blessing of other people in our lives?

- How can you be there for others facing what you are facing?

A THREATENING STORM

"From there Elisha went up to Bethel. As he was walking up the path, some small boys came out of the city and harassed him, chanting, 'Go up, baldy! Go up, baldy.'" *2 Kings 2:23 (HCSB)*

*K*atrina tore up the low-lying areas of Louisiana, puncturing levees and weakening structures along the way. The monster storm disrupted and destroyed lives in a way few storms have done before. Yet the hurricane season didn't end after Katrina and a few weeks later, another devastating storm formed in the Atlantic and intensified in the Gulf of Mexico. As the storm progressed, the same areas wrecked by Katrina lay in the path of Rita (2005).

The threat of Rita led to urgent calls for preparation and evacuations. Though work had been performed on the levee system, a storm of Rita's size and strength could again lead to catastrophic flooding and loss of life. Residents and meteorologists focused on the exact track the storm took as it bore down on the mainland. The threat caused people to tune out the trivial trappings of daily life to focus on what was heading their way.

The realization of a threat shifts our attention. We brace for what may come.

Threats fill the air on a grander scale in our world today. Whether it be the threats on social media to the ones issued in the middle of an argument, there are threats everywhere. Streets are more dangerous than before, and life finds its share of threats within the slightest misunderstandings between people.

As Elisha traveled, a group threatened the man of God. As they called out, their words were not only ridiculing but also threatening. The numbers alone said that Elisha was in danger as he was only one man and there were at least forty-two of them calling out to him. But Who was on Elisha's side stood far bigger than the threat that rose up against him that day.

Elisha continued to walk. As he walked, they screamed even louder. Elisha knew that danger lurked, that their words were more than empty taunts. The threats elicited a response from Elisha as he turned and called out a curse on those who intended to harm him. When he did, they met a cruel fate. Bears emerged and mauled those who posed the threat to the man of God. God had a purpose for Elisha, and no one was going to stop the Lord's plan.

Storms of threats take place all the time. Though some threats are easily dismissed, others must be taken more seriously. Some threats are spoken from a heart intent on following through. Threatening storms keep us on edge, but the presence of the Lord helps calm our fear of those threats.

Hebrews points out that if the Lord is with us, we do not have to fear the workings or the threats of man. It says, "Therefore, we may boldly say: The Lord is my helper; I will not be afraid. What can man do to me?" (Hebrews 13:6 HCSB) Threats may come, but our security comes from One bigger than any threat. We need to be aware when the threats of life come and prepare daily for their arrival, but we cannot live in fear of such a storm. The Lord can silence the threats today just as He did in Elisha's day.

Storm Preparation

- What are the worst threats you have had in your life?

- What do we learn about threatening people from the story of Elisha?

- How does faith calm the thundering storm of threats in our lives?

THE PERFECT STORM

"However, Jonah got up to flee to Tarshish from the Lord's presence. He went down to Joppa and found a ship going to Tarshish. He paid the fare and went down into it to go with them to Tarshish, from the Lord's presence." *Jonah 1:3 (HCSB)*

Sebastian Junger's book, and the film that came later starring George Clooney, highlighted what some have called The Perfect Storm. The storm absorbed the remnants of another storm, Hurricane Grace (1991), and churned in the open waters. The storm is one of the most well-known storms because of the spotlight placed on it by Hollywood, but its story is one of caution and tragedy.

One of the most startling measurements of the storm was a wave measured at one hundred feet. Surge and high winds affected many in the coastal areas. The story of the Andrea Gail raised awareness of the storm as the fishing vessel sank and the ocean claimed the lives of all those on board.

The elements of the storm are a rare phenomenon. The timing brought the systems on a collision course and, thus, the perfect storm emerged.

Life storms emerge all the time. There are some, however, that distinguish themselves. A perfect storm in life is one that holds the ability to swallow us if the right decisions are not made. When those storms hit, the outcome can truly hang on what choice we make.

Jonah's story is one of a perfect storm. God spoke to Jonah and gave him directions. The prophet, however, chose to go in the opposite direction. Jonah disagreed with what the Lord told him to do as he harbored bitterness towards the Ninevites. So, Jonah ignored the Lord and ran away from God's calling on that day. The decision made by Jonah set off a chain of events that led to a monster storm in his life.

The very trajectory of his life changed. When you read the opening of the book of Jonah, God is speaking to Jonah and is planning to use Jonah for something great. To hear from God and to be chosen by God for a work of God is one of the greatest levels to arrive at in life. Jonah could not see this blessing on his life from where he sat that day, so he rebelled. What jumps off the page is how quickly his life turned in a different direction.

In the first chapter, we read of a downward spiral that began at the moment of his rejection. He went down to Joppa to go down to Tarshish. He went down into the ship. After the Lord hurled a storm, Jonah was tossed overboard, and he went down into the waters before going down in the belly of the fish.

Jonah chose his will over God's will and a storm began brewing. What Jonah experienced and what he caused others to endure could have been avoided by listening to God and following through with what God called him to do. He didn't, and a storm was unleashed. Jonah found grace as the Lord gave him a second chance to do what was right, what he was called to do initially.

When we rebel against God, we can begin looking for a storm to come. Because of His great love for us, He doesn't allow us to stay in rebellion but draws us back to him. Hebrews 12 says, "My son, do not take the Lord's discipline lightly or faint when you are reproved by Him, for the Lord disciplines the one He loves and punishes every son He receives." (Hebrews 12:5–6 HCSB) One surefire way to avoid a perfect storm in life is to stay inside the will of God. As Jonah learned, getting outside the will of the Lord leads to rough times and threatening waters.

Storm Preparation

- What storm in your life came as a result of your defiance of God?

- Why do you think the Lord hurled all he did at Jonah when Jonah ran away?

- What do we learn from Jonah?

A DEADLY STORM

"If the God we serve exists, then He can rescue us from the furnace of blazing fire, and He can rescue us for the power of you, the king. But even if He does not rescue us, we want you as king to know that we will not serve your gods or worship the gold statue you set up."
Daniel 3:17–18 (HCSB)

*b*uildings and houses can be replaced. A death, however, leaves a void that cannot be filled because a life cannot be replaced. Of all the costs of a hurricane's landfall, the loss of life stands as the costliest of all. Hurricane Ike (2008) proved to be a deadly storm, claiming the lives of far too many people.

Ike peaked as a Category 4 hurricane as it traveled from the Atlantic to the Gulf of Mexico. Along its path, the terrifying storm claimed the lives of nearly two hundred people. The concentration of the highest number of fatalities was in the United States while Haiti also experienced many deaths. The deadly storm of 2008 reminds everyone that we have no guarantee of life beyond the moment we are given.

Of all the fears in this world, death stands as the number one fear in most people. A storm that appears to end in death is a storm that shakes most people. We do all we can to avoid anything that promises or even threatens to be deadly. How do we stand when it feels like the storm will cause us to perish?

The thought of death causes most to adopt a new behavior, to change their mind, or even to compromise. Our typical thought process is to preserve life as long as possible. We champion that which promises to help us live a longer life, and we take care of the things that might cause us to have a shorter time on this earth. Shadrach, Meshach, and Abednego faced a storm that led to what appeared to be guaranteed death. They defied the king's order, and the punishment was to be thrown into a fiery furnace. The king offered them another chance. If they wanted to ensure life, all they had to do was bow to the statue and escape the sentence handed down to them previously.

In the storm of a death sentence, most would jump at the chance of a pardon. Not these three. They refused. Before you assume they knew the Lord would deliver them, look back at their own words. They explained to the king that a possibility existed that God would allow them to perish in the flames. Even so, they refused to bow down, unwavering in their determination not to compromise their convictions.

Why? Why would they not back down though a deadly storm bore down on them? They could have said that God gave them the way out with a second chance to bow, but they knew such a justification would be a lie. Those who realize that living for God and living for what exists beyond this life leave the fear of death behind. Faith says that what comes after this life is better. Shadrach, Meshach, and Abednego would rather die with their convictions in place than live another day as compromisers without integrity. The apostle Paul said, "For me, living is Christ and dying is gain." (Philippians 1:21 HCSB) He knew something greater awaited when this life ended. Paul, like Shadrach, Meshach, and Abednego, knew that living this life must be done righteously, living by faith, and none feared death as much as they feared compromising what they truly believed.

Why do we fear the storms that seem to lead too close to death for comfort? Do we place more value on this life or what comes after? Faith says we have nothing to fear because life in heaven is worth looking forward to daily. In Christ, there is the assurance of eternal life. That assurance led Christians to give their lives for the gospel in other regions of the world. Though we currently face such a storm only on rare occasions, the Bible tells us that these storms will come. We must prepare today as if that storm may strike tomorrow.

Storm Preparation

- How does the attitude of the three inspire you to stand firm in life?
- What calms your fear about eternal life when a deadly storm threatens?
- What Bible verses tell us not to fear death?

Image © iStock.com/stevegee

THE IMPOSSIBLE STORM

"Isn't this what we told you in Egypt: Leave us alone so that we may serve the Egyptians? It would have been better for us to serve the Egyptians than to die in the wilderness." Exodus 14:12 (HCSB)

*h*urricanes typically take a similar path as far as where they experience growth, and there are places where hurricanes are much less likely to develop. A great number start as a wave off the coast of Africa, building strength and energy over the open waters of the Atlantic. Others begin in the Caribbean Sea or the Gulf of Mexico, taking aim on Central America, Mexico, or the states bordering the Gulf of Mexico. The area closer to the equator typically doesn't lead to great formation of a storm, but there are exceptions.

Hurricane Ivan (2004) defied the norms of major hurricane formation. Ivan's development so far south set records for the southernmost Category 3 storm and later set the record for the southernmost Category 4 storm. No history suggested the storm could grow as rapidly, but sometimes the impossible proves itself to be possible.

There are areas of life that seem to be safe havens, the very areas where no storm could strike. The very history of our lives says that it is impossible not to know this, where we say a storm could never strike is the very area where one can churn up.

The Egyptians grew accustomed to having the Hebrews serve them. The plagues came and afterwards, the Hebrews were given the freedom to leave. Moses led the children of Israel out of bondage, but shortly thereafter, Pharaoh changed his mind and gave chase. With the Red Sea ahead, the Egyptian army had the children of Israel trapped. Nothing could stop the recapturing of the formerly oppressed people.

The Red Sea promised to be the perfect barrier for the Egyptians until the Lord accomplished what only He could accomplish. A powerful east wind came, splitting the sea so the children of Israel could pass through, escaping the army closing in. The wind blew as long as they were crossing. After they reached the other side, the winds subsided, and the Egyptian army in pursuit perished. The Egyptians never imagined being swept away in such a manner.

Never had anyone witnessed such an event. Hemmed in, the children of Israel were doomed to recapture. However, the impossible unfolded as the Lord made a way for His people to escape. God hurled a wind that opened a way out.

Life closes in and, when we feel encircled, the feeling of no way out takes over. We feel that it is impossible to overcome and that we will be conquered instead of being more than conquerors. We fall in a hole too deep to escape on our own. Down at the bottom, in the darkness, there is only one place to look to find light: up.

If you are feeling hemmed in by life right now, look to see how God is making a way of escape for you today. The impossible may be brewing on your behalf. On the other hand, make sure you are pursuing the right things, or He might send a seemingly impossible storm to stop your pursuit of what you need to stop pursuing.

Storm Preparation

- What are you pursuing in your life right now—is it something God will help you obtain or is it something that He will stop you from pursuing?

- How did the impossible storm benefit the children of God? How did it hurt the Egyptians?

- What determined the outcome between the children of Israel and the Egyptians? Why did one storm have such a different impact on two groups of people?

A POWERFUL STORM

"But if it doesn't please you to worship Yahweh, choose for yourselves today the one you will worship: the gods your fathers worshipped beyond the Euphrates River or the gods of the Amorites in whose land you are living. As for me and my family, we will worship Yahweh."
Joshua 24:15 (HCSB)

*t*he Atlantic Ocean never saw a storm as intense as the hurricane spawned in the latter half of October 2005. Wilma's approach to the Yucatan Peninsula brought fear as the hurricane exploded into a Category 5, threatening lives and properties. The sudden burst took it from a minimal threat to an overwhelming risk in only a day.

Wilma had the most intense pressure of any Atlantic hurricane. Power and fury marked Wilma's presence as she plowed into Mexico's Yucatan, veered almost 90 degrees, returned to the Gulf, re-intensified over water, and struck the southern portion of Florida before heading out into the Atlantic on a northeasterly course. Mexico took the hardest hit, and Wilma ensured it would be a storm for the history books. At one point, Wilma's sustained winds were 185 miles per hour with a pressure of 882 millibars.

Our Lady of Lourdes Grotto drew many in Key West to pray for the storm to move away, for the protection of the islands. The power of the storm prompted many people to turn to a greater power in advance of the storm's approach—they turned to the power of God.

A storm rages in our lives quite frequently. The storm comes from the struggle as to what has true power in our lives. Have you ever found yourself in a raging storm that threatened to overpower you and derail your life? Joshua stood before the people and asked them who held the power in their lives. They had options. They could serve the gods in the land where they dwelt. Bowing down to other gods that their fathers served was another option. Or they could serve the true and living God. They had options, but Joshua forced the people to choose one.

Joshua proclaimed that he and his family served God. He chose what He knew to be real, committing before all men where his allegiance stood. Regardless of anyone else's choice, his choice, his family's choice, was made. Joshua understood the power of the Living God and ensured his family knew Who held the greatest power. His dedication pushed others to dedicate their lives as well.

The power of storms in life sends us in one of two directions—we either run for our lives or we run to the Source of life. Ultimate power is found in the direction we run at the moment we realize we need that power in our lives. If the world holds the power, we will look to the world for guidance, help, and strength. But if we believe God to be on His throne, we turn to

Him with the understanding that no storm in history has held more power than He holds.

Who do you serve and is the one you serve truly powerful? Life hurls winds and rains, but with a word, the Lord can calm any storm. If you are battered, or if you are facing a storm too big for you, turn to the One bigger than the storm.

Storm Preparation

- Why does Joshua's decision inspire us today?

- What storm in your life stood too tall for you but not too big for God?

- How does understanding God's power help us better face storms?

RESCUE OTHERS *in* THEIR STORM

"For the Son of Man has come to seek and to save the lost."
Luke 19:10 (HCSB)

urricane Dorian devastated the Bahamas during the 2019 hurricane season. The Category 5 storm destroyed Grand Bahama Island and other areas. Billions of dollars in damages resulted from the bullseye the storm scored on the islands. Winds of more than 180 miles per hour, with gusts up to 200 miles per hour, flattened buildings. The thought of what the storm could bring fell short of what actually happened as the storm lashed out over a full day. Many interviewed for television and newspapers mentioned how they lost all they had in Dorian's devastation.

One of the stories that came from Dorian was the work of the United

States Coast Guard. Though the members of the Coast Guard were safe and out of harm's way, they sprang into action for those in danger, those who needed rescuing after Dorian. The Coast Guard ran missions to the islands to rescue those who needed help desperately.

With each helicopter flight, they pulled people out of the rubble. Destitute individuals found the necessities lacking in their devastated hometowns, things like food and clean drinking water. The Coast Guard undertook to reach out to those who had nowhere to go and no one to turn to in their desperation.

As we look at storms, we open our eyes not only to the storms in our lives, but we also note the storms others must endure. We see the storm they're in and we are moved to action. We go where the need is because that's what Jesus did.

One day, He traveled through Jericho and paused to speak to a man hated by those of his community. Zacchaeus climbed a tree to see Jesus. Too short to see over the crowd, he searched for a way to catch a glimpse. People considered him to be a pariah as his job allowed him to cheat people, and cheating people lined his pockets. A storm raged inside Zacchaeus as he had almost anything he wanted but in Jesus, he encountered someone very different.

Jesus looked up and spoke. He reached out to the one in a tree. When He called, Zacchaeus came running. When He spoke, all those who heard then knew the mission of Jesus' life, the mission for our lives too. Jesus said that He came to seek and to save the lost. He encountered a multitude of people going through a wide range of storms. He was their rescue.

We have learned how to handle the storms of life. Now, we are called to lead rescue missions to others in the storms of their lives. As they fight to endure the storm, we have the perfect chance to step in and lead them to their rescuer, Jesus Christ. When a storm destroys their lives, we can help them pick up and rebuild while pointing them to Christ who can put life back together. Paul had such an attitude in his life when it came to others. He wrote to the Corinthians, "To the weak I became weak, in order to win the weak. I have become all things to all people, so that I may by every possible means save some." (1 Corinthians 9:20 HCSB)

We all face storms, and we all can be there for others in their storms. What we learn from our storms can help others and what we are called to do can help others survive their own storms.

Storm Preparation

- How does the work of the Coast Guard in the aftermath of Hurricane Dorian inspire you?
- How can we put the mission of Jesus in action during someone else's life storm?
- Name a time Jesus rescued you.

CONCLUSION

*e*very year, another hurricane season arrives. Activity in the tropics draws the attention of meteorologists and people throughout the world. New storms will form. Lives will be impacted. And with each passing year, we will study the storms and attempt to prepare better than we had in previous years.

Just as there is an assurance of a hurricane season, we know storms will rage in our lives while we are here on this earth. The calm waters of today are stirred by events, circumstances, and situations. It is my hope that now after we have looked at the Bible and the storms we face in life, we are prepared to weather the storms better than ever before.

In the Sermon on the Mount, Jesus assured the crowd that storms were inevitable. They come and they pound against us, often without mercy or warning. But Jesus ensured the crowd that day that they would understand how to make it through those storms. He said to them, "Therefore, everyone who hears these words of Mine and acts on them will be like a sensible man who built his house on the rock. The rains fell, the rivers rose, and the winds blew and pounded that house. Yet it didn't collapse because its foundation was on the rock." (Matthew 7:24–25 HCSB)

Build a foundation on Him so that when the storms come, you know you will make it through by His hand. When storms rise up, let faith rise up even higher. The storms throw all they have at us, but with Jesus, we have all that we will ever need to remain standing.

When we look back at all the storms we have endured in life and we see how the Lord brought us through each one, we stand in awe of Him. As you continue to walk with Him each day of your life, be in awe of the size and power of your God rather than being fearful of the size of the storm that is raging.

God has made a way. He did for Noah, and He has for you. Use what He teaches you to help someone else in their storm of life and praise the Lord for the opportunity. You are here. He has you here for a reason and, with every storm, He brings us through, He strengthens our faith a little bit more as we realize that He is more than able.

May God bless you. May He give you the strength and the wisdom that you need each day as you live for His glory. Praise Him for every break in the clouds and tell others of the God who has delivered you from the raging storms of your life.

ACKNOWLEDGMENTS

i want to thank the Lord for this opportunity. I am deeply appreciative of the many times He has delivered me from the storms of life. Without Him, I would be nothing, so I thank Jesus for all He is to me.

I want to thank my wife and my children for all of their understanding and their love and support. Crystal, thank you for all you do. Cheyenne, Autumn, and Brady—God blessed me deeply with the three of you.

A special thanks goes to End Game Press. Thank you for taking a chance on me and on this idea. To Victoria Duerstock—you amaze me. I know few other people on this earth who inspire me as much as you do.

Thank you to my agent and my friend, Cyle Young. I deeply appreciate the investment you have made in my life. Thank you to all the Serious Writer Family. I am truly honored to be associated with all of you. To Michelle Medlock Adams and Bethany Jett—thank you for your guidance and support. Thank you, Del Duduit, for your friendship and support.

Thank you to my parents and my family. Each of you have helped me achieve more in this life than I would have achieved on my own. Thank you to my church, Mt. Zion Baptist, as your support means so much.

To my friends—I cannot thank you enough. To have the friends that I have is truly to be a blessed man. So, to the whole crew, I say thank you.

Finally, I thank you, the reader. You didn't have to purchase this, but it is my prayer that something inside these pages has encouraged you. If it has, give the Lord the credit and live it out each day.